D0368246

BORN EXTRAORDINARY

Empowering Children with Differences and Disabilities

MEG ZUCKER

A TarcherPerigee Book

tarcherperigee

an imprint of Penguin Random House LLC
penguinrandomhouse.com

TarcherPerigee with tp colophon is a registered trademark of Penguin Random House LLC.

Most TarcherPerigee books are available at special quantity discounts for bulk purchase for sales promotions, premiums, fund-raising, and educational needs. Special books or book excerpts also can be created to fit specific needs. For details, write: SpecialMarkets@penguinrandomhouse.com.

Library of Congress Cataloging-in-Publication Data

Names: Zucker, Meg, author.
Title: Born extraordinary: empowering children with differences and disabilities / Meg Zucker.
Description: New York: TarcherPerigee, 2023.
Identifiers: LCCN 2022033415 (print) | LCCN 2022033416 (ebook) |
ISBN 9780593419380 (trade paperback) | ISBN 9780593419397 (epub)
Subjects: LCSH: Parents of children with disabilities. |
Children with disabilities. | Self-esteem in children. | Parenting.
Classification: LCC HQ759.913.Z83 2023 (print) | LCC HQ759.913 (ebook) |
DDC 649/.15—dc23/eng/20220824
LC record available at https://lccn.loc.gov/2022033415
LC ebook record available at https://lccn.loc.gov/2022033416

Printed in the United States of America
1st Printing

Book design by Laura K. Corless

Some names and identifying details have been changed to protect the privacy of individuals.

Praise for *Born Extraordinary*

"Meg Zucker has written a warmhearted, practical guide to navigating a world that can all too often lack empathy and understanding. Her honesty and wisdom, drawn from a deep well of lived experience, will not only empower kids with disabilities but their parents and caregivers, too."

—Emily Ladau, author of *Demystifying Disability*

"Validating and empowering, *Born Extraordinary* is just the companionable guide every parent of a kid with differences and disabilities needs. Mixing real-life experiences with compassion, humor, and practical advice, Meg Zucker affirms that your child is absolutely right, just as they are—and supports you in helping them thrive. This book is an invaluable guide with authentic stories and actionable strategies. I wish I'd had a copy years ago!"

—Heather Lanier, author of *Raising a Rare Girl*

"In *Born Extraordinary*, Meg Zucker delivers a profound set of lessons to guide families raising kids who are different or disabled. Drawing on personal experience, Meg guides parents to help their children and themselves adapt, find peace, and experience confidence and self-love. Meg shows us that differences are a blessing."

—Mallika Chopra, author of *Just Breathe*

"*Born Extraordinary* should be required reading for all pediatricians and parents. Meg Zucker shows us that, given the appropriate framework, children with either visible or invisible differences can and should thrive despite their challenges."

—Brenda Anders Pring, MD,
Fellow of the American Academy of Pediatrics

This book is dedicated to my parents, Francine and Marvin Weinbaum, who intuitively empowered me to reach my greatest potential. And to my loving husband, John Zucker, who joined me in guiding our children to achieve the same.

CONTENTS

PREFACE

To the complete shock of my parents, I was born with only one finger on each hand, shortened forearms, and one toe on each misshapen tiny stump of a foot. Whether I would be able to walk, write, or function in any normal capacity was, at best, up in the air. The doctors couldn't reassure them of anything, or even offer a medical term for my condition. Everyone was out of their depth, and there was no book on the shelf to guide or help my parents cope. Everything that had felt important prior to this day diminished in comparison.

Upon hearing the news about my disfigured body, a dear friend of my parents, novelist Elizabeth Klein (Shapiro), appreciated that in such circumstances, "Is there anything I can do?" would be empty and meaningless. Her friends' world had been turned upside down, and there was no turning back. So instead, Elizabeth provided them with the one thing every parent needs when their child is born different or becomes different: perspective.

We Are All Born Lacking
by Elizabeth Klein

Into this world of appurtenances
You have come, unequipped
To walk on water, to perform
The laying on of hands. In that sweet
Face lies all your stock.
Wares to wear down neat doctrines
Of perfection, alter your parents'
Pain.
I pray
While your mother doubts
Direction, your father
Silences regret.
I pray our gentle being
Will make hands, feet—
The appendages of body—no more than grace notes
On a printed score,
Embellishments, ornamental trills,
Unessential to the music's inner life
Which swells and falls to the skill
Of the musician. May your spirit dance
On invisible toes. Dear one,
We are all born lacking.

BORN
EXTRAORDINARY

INTRODUCTION

The first time I learned that my genetic condition had a name was when I was at a medical exam when I was applying to law school. My doctor was completing a required form for me, and on the final line, he wrote something unrecognizable: ectrodactyly.

"What's that?" I asked, staring at the piece of paper, confused.

To me, the word sounded more like a type of dinosaur. And when he explained it was simply a medical term rooted in Greek that meant missing digits, I felt a surge of disappointment. Telling me I was limb different wasn't exactly news. And I was on my own on this adventure since neither my parents, brothers, nor any relative shared my condition. When I was growing up and other kids constantly asked why I looked so different, I'd explain that I was born this way, and my mom had eaten some spoiled fish while pregnant with me. It was as good as any guess, so I stuck to it for years.

Growing up, I'd never met anyone who looked like me—not in person, not on television, not even in my wildest dreams.

Well, maybe once. The closest I'd ever come was on one hot summer evening at a county fair in central Illinois. Among the carnival rides and games, there was also a freak show with people on display. It included a pair of conjoined twins, a bearded lady, and a middle-aged man with missing fingers and toes. I stared at him in horror, and in response, he stared back at me. But before he looked away, he offered a nod with a strange expression, as if to say, "You're like me."

What would have been more useful, however, was if my doctor could have let me in on the news that my condition was not only genetic, but also autosomal dominant. That meant I had a 50 percent chance of passing ectrodactyly on to my children. Now *that* would have mattered. For much of my youth and into my twenties, I chose to remain in denial, believing that my genetic mishap would start and end with me. Why? My greatest fear was passing it along to my offspring; they would blame me, and I would blame myself. When I shared that with my now husband, John, before we got engaged, he pooh-poohed me.

"Geez, Meg, what are you so afraid of? You came out great, and even if our kids inherit it, they will follow your lead."

I have my own mom and dad to thank for that. Their unconditional support has shaped the confident person and unwavering parent I've become.

Although I was born in the United States, much of my childhood was spent in five countries across the Middle East and South Asia. There, my ability to be resilient was constantly tested. When we moved to Iran, beggars on the street would run for the hills, worried they might catch my condition or my family's presumed curse. When I lived in Cairo, Egypt, and Islamabad, Pakistan, people would pass me on the street and let out loud murmurs of pity. In Kabul, Afghanistan, my own nanny was afraid of me. But there were upsides to my experiences abroad. In Israel, we lived in an apartment, and our landlady was named Regina. She had moved from Wisconsin to Jerusalem with her best friend, named Golda Meir, who later became the prime minister. One day Golda was visiting Regina and saw me playing outside. She stopped before entering the building, stared at my small, disfigured hands for a moment, and then whispered in my ear:

"You are enough."

I was startled by her boldness. Up until that moment, any stranger that had ever encountered me had only shown uncertainty, fear, or pity. Although I was too young to fully appreciate it, Golda sought to reassure me that no matter what I looked like, I would get through a lifetime of pity, stares, and false assumptions about my abilities just by being me. Her words would one day capture my own life commitment to unconditional self-love. And yet, as important as the encouragement was, it would be up to my parents to help me believe it, because when the world takes one glance at you and reminds you of everything you aren't, you need to rely on constant reinforcement at home to remind you of everything you are.

As it turned out, my prayers of not passing on ectrodactyly went unheeded. Ethan was born with one finger on each hand and two toes on each foot, and a few years later, his brother Charlie was born with two fingers on each hand and two toes on each foot. There wasn't much of a chance that their younger sister, Savanna, would share our genetic condition because she was adopted at birth. Even so, Savanna would have her own invisible differences. Beyond the adoption, she developed a severe allergy to nuts and would later be diagnosed with attention deficit hyperactivity disorder (ADHD).

Altogether, thanks to my genetics, Ethan, Charlie, and I have eighteen fingers and toes combined. I'll let that sink in for a minute. In my case, the cause was certain, so I used to think I was uniquely tormented by the guilt of our sons being born different. But in speaking to countless parents, I have come to realize I am hardly alone. My own mother tells me that she was tortured by a pediatrician who suggested that had she not eaten a rotten potato chip early in her pregnancy with me, I'd have been born genetically perfect. And to think I'd told all the other kids that it had been some bad fish. My mother agonized over that clueless diagnosis for years. But here's the thing. As is the case for many new parents, the initial feelings of guilt over having a child that is different transforms into unimaginable gushes of love and affection. Elizabeth Bruenig described motherhood in a *New York Times* piece in a way that resonated with me: "One of the things they don't tell you about having babies is that you don't ever have *a* baby; you have *your* baby, which is to you . . . the sum of all babies."

Despite the fact that two of our three children share my condition, I quickly realized I had so much to learn. Parenting children who were born different was actually not intuitive, not even for me! My parents had done such a brilliant job of raising me to take control and conquer, both emotionally and physically, to the best of my ability; how I wished they would have written a guidebook for *me* to follow. They raised me to be fearlessly independent and follow my passions, no matter what. Had they written a book, it would have highlighted the importance of "leaning out" by resisting the urge to overprotect or prevent me from ever experiencing failure, while never sharing any private reservations about what might or might not be feasible. I blossomed in response. All it takes is a nervous, panicky parent to cause a reluctant child to become apprehensive about trying new things and give up before they've given themselves a chance.

As a person who is different and as a mother of children who are different, I'm writing this book to give you the key ingredients necessary to help your child, who was born different or experiences challenges as a result of real or perceived differences, to live to their greatest potential. As a parent, you must achieve unconditional self-love before focusing on being the parent they'll need; you'll need to help your child find their dignity in public while providing them the support they'll hunger for at home; you can't make decisions on their behalf based on fear—you need to resist the urge to overprotect while finding the courage to follow their lead; you'll need to preserve their pride as they yearn to be independent despite a world that perceives them as helpless; you'll discover the benefits of family support that flows both ways; and you'll need to help your children discern between cruelty and curiosity while preparing them for anything.

In *Born Extraordinary*, I share successful approaches as well as my mistakes so that parents have the right tools to empower children who are either born physically different or become physically different along the way. As founder and president of

Don't Hide It, Flaunt It, a 501(c)(3) nonprofit whose mission is to unite people around unconditionally accepting and celebrating *all* differences, I believe that parents whose children struggle with unseen or invisible challenges will find many of the lessons in this book to be beneficial as well. Finally, *Born Extraordinary* also provides valuable insight for parents who simply wish to raise inclusive and empathetic children. We all shudder at the thought of our child embarrassing anyone (including ourselves) with a loud outburst upon seeing someone they perceive as different. While not every lesson will be applicable for all, there will be useful nuggets throughout, and you can pick and choose which feel most appropriate for your family. Beyond my own family's experiences, I have included many sage words of wisdom from other parents similarly raising children with visible and invisible differences of all kinds. Their personal stories are incorporated throughout, including many compiled in the "Additional Words of Wisdom" section at the end of the book.

The expression "Wash, rinse, repeat" comes to mind when I think about how I've worked for years to champion my children's abilities and support their emotional needs, just like my parents did for me. Thankfully, with patience, courage, and commitment, success is not only achievable, but it's ours for the taking.

WHY "DIFFERENT"?

You might wonder why I am not referring to myself and our sons as disabled throughout the book. For years I struggled with the term, not directly identifying with it. To me, the word was anchored in the concept of *limitation*. My parents, however, raised me to believe that the world was my oyster, that I should have the opportunity to try anything I wish in life. As Golda reminded me, I was enough. In that sense, I never knew any different and therefore never saw myself as limited. And so I equated the word "disabled" with unfortunate or incapable. Then one morning I was again reminded why I didn't want the word "disabled" associated with me or my children. As I was shuffling around getting ready to go to work, I heard a traffic report on the news cautioning us all to steer clear of a highway. Why? We would be delayed by a disabled car. The following morning, I paid closer attention to yet another reporter describing a different accident and saying that our commute would be "ruined by a *disabled* vehicle on the road." And so, the term unfortunately still has negative connotations.

Then again, there are certainly many amazing people who believe the term "disabled" is something to enthusiastically adopt and embrace. They literally fly the flag of disability pride. I'm not here to persuade anyone to change the language they use to describe themselves or their children, but for the purposes of this book, the word "different" is used in a generic way to describe anyone who is considered atypical and therefore feels judged by society as outside the norm.

CHAPTER 1

Embracing the New Normal

I've often heard people use the expression "My world was turned upside down" to describe incidents as frivolous as finding out their favorite hairdresser moved to another state. But the phrase is intended to capture something that is truly shocking or upsetting. To me, it is aptly applied when your child arrives or unexpectedly becomes different. Embracing your new normal is not a sprint but a marathon. And whether the news comes when you are pregnant or later on, it is easy to be tortured by guilt. As my own mother described it after having me, she felt almost insane with anguish. That got me thinking about what types of feelings a parent can expect when their child is born different. It can start out rough, mimicking the stages of grief: Shock and denial, pain and guilt, anger, bargaining, and possibly depression, but then comes the upward turn. You begin to work through your family's new normal—finally arriving at acceptance and hope. In the end, you'll even come to appreciate that the experience provided a deep level of fulfillment you hadn't been seeking and didn't even realize you were lacking. As with anything worthwhile, your struggle, and rising to the occasion, will be joyfully rewarded. Your child's difference will even become something to celebrate.

But first things first.

HOW LOW I SANK

I think it's important for me to first take a step back and describe my own personal fears and struggles when faced with the reality that I'd be a parent of a child who was different. While all that pain is thankfully behind me, it's impossible to fully appreciate how far I've come without learning how low I sank. And if you're feeling down at this moment, know you are not alone and there is a light at the end of what feels like a dark and ominous tunnel.

A few months after John and I got engaged, he understandably wanted to make sure we saw a specialist to ensure we were fully informed before trying to start a family. Although he suspected my condition was genetic, he also didn't make it a deal breaker. Yes, I know John's a keeper. I've had the good fortune of marrying a man who has tolerated my whims and, most important, loved me unconditionally long before I felt that way about myself. I reluctantly agreed to go to the geneticist, but still tried to convince him that our children wouldn't share my condition. How was I so certain? Because before I met John, instead of poring through books on ectrodactyly or dominant gene mutations, I received the assurance I needed . . . from a psychic named Reese. I had graduated from law school the year before and was sitting in the front room of her tiny apartment on 14th Street and First Avenue in New York City, when she said, "You will have two children and they won't have your handicap."

Her pronouncement was music to my ears. Tears began to stream down my cheeks. Although I had found the word "handicap" to be both dated and personally offensive, I chose to ignore it. Reese insisted I pay her in cash before we sat at a small table in the front room and she shuffled a deck of tarot cards. In her late forties, Reese was quite pretty, with olive-colored skin and long black hair wrapped in a scarf over the top. I'd endure anything to hear someone tell me that my children would be born perfect.

"Are you sure?" I asked weakly.

I trembled, afraid she couldn't really predict the future but desperately wanting her to be right. I asked Reese to repeat her vision.

"Come back next week."

And so I did, again and again. Given my accomplishments to date, these weekly visits were quite ironic. On my way home from my plum job at a premier financial firm on Wall Street, I'd visit Reese to hear that everything would be all right. So as my career was taking flight, I'd never been more pathetic.

Each week that I visited Reese, she would select different tarot cards. But when it was time to examine them, she'd always pause and beam at me.

"The cards never lie. You will marry and have two children; neither of them will be born with your hands."

Reese stared at one of the cards for a long moment, then my

hands, and then looked away. Apparently, she hadn't noticed my feet. I made a mental note to ask her about them to make sure I wouldn't pass on that part of my condition, either. I never thought I'd been addicted to anything, but reflecting back, Reese's predictions were the very drug that eased my deepest dread. In fact, I felt so indebted to her that after the first month, I decided paying her weekly wasn't sufficient. On one occasion, I gave her an envelope with a gift certificate to an exclusive spa day at Elizabeth Arden's Red Door Spa on the Upper East Side. On another occasion, we met downtown near Wall Street at the discounted luxury brand department store, Century 21. There, she introduced me to her grown son. Reese had explained that buying him an expensive leather coat that he badly needed was the least I could do.

Back at the Mount Sinai consultation with John, the doctor turned to me and frowned, informing me that my condition was genetic and I had a 50 percent chance of passing it on to our children.

I was crushed at first. But then, attempting to reassure myself, I rationalized the unwelcome news.

I thought to myself, "Even if it's genetic, I'll simply land on the right side of the equation. That must have been why Reese saw that everything would work out."

The following year, I became pregnant with our firstborn, Ethan.

At our first medical appointment at around the eight-week gestational period, we heard the heartbeat and John practically jumped out of his seat in joy. This was particularly momentous because we'd had two prior miscarriages and had never come that far. While John was all smiles, though, my nerves began swinging into motion. Was Reese really able to predict the digit-count of my future children? Would my baby inherit my condition? At the nineteen-week anatomy scan at Mount Sinai Hospital on the Upper East Side, I'd have my answer.

"He has a very healthy-looking heart. It is beating perfectly."

Fifteen minutes earlier, I had hoisted my enlarged pregnant body onto the examination table and braced for the cold gel. The hospital technician had been gliding the hard plastic wand all over my abdomen while staring at the black-and-white screen with a silhouette of our unborn son.

"The brain size and shape are normal. You should be in the clear, just a few more things to check . . ."

Initially, she had been smiling pleasantly. But then her expression darkened.

"Is everything okay?" I asked blithely. John placed his hand firmly on my leg as if to say, "Just wait."

"Excuse me, I'll be right back."

She had failed miserably at masking her concerned expression, leaving me lying there with John by my side. A few minutes later, the doctor walked in and placed the wand over the same areas as the technician.

"I'm sorry to be the one to tell you both this, but we can only find one finger on each hand . . . and two toes on each foot."

He stared at my own hands and shortened forearms and added, "I presume you both knew the risks."

Then, as if to offer a bright side, "The baby does, however, seem to have normal-length forearms. Want to know the gender?"

My own parents had given me insight that when a child is born different, a dark cloud colors the birthing room. Faces drop. An awkward silence fills the air. If someone thinks to congratulate you, there is hesitation in their voice. No one really knows what to say, not even you. All the movies I'd seen with everyone utterly relieved the newborn baby had ten fingers and ten toes flashed before my eyes. The news that Ethan would be born different was devastating, my life's greatest fear now realized.

OVERCOMING THE GUILT

In the beginning, when a baby is born different, one word comes into focus: loss. Loss of the picture-perfect family. Loss of the ability to show off your baby with instant pride. Loss of that anticipated bond with close friends who can no longer fully relate. Loss of the privilege of worrying about the unimportant things in life. Loss of confidence and any clear picture of how to parent. Loss of conversations with family and friends starting light instead of heavy and concerned. Loss of an easier life.

The guilt of not having been able to take control and prevent your new reality is raw and real. When my mother gave birth to me during a blizzard, the storm outside felt calm compared to how she felt internally. Despite feeling innate motherly love, she also felt, as she described it, out of her mind with emotional pain and guilt every time she looked at my hands and feet. She was so personally tortured that my dad mainly took care of me during my first year while she cared for my older brother, Peter.

"What if I would have zigged instead of zagged? Maybe then you would've been born *perfect*."

And as for me, feeling at fault doesn't even begin to describe it. Unlike most people who understand that getting pregnant can involve risks, mine were more than speculative. With Ethan born and my biggest fear realized, I couldn't help but think of my own mother's traumatic experience and how deeply she blamed herself. I could now relate.

Yet, I got through it. But how?

If only there's a decisive epiphany waiting around the corner, like someone smacking you and barking, "Snap out of it!" as Loretta (Cher) exploded at Ronny (Nicolas Cage) in the film *Moonstruck*. If only life were that simple. No, instead I began to think a lot about my father's favorite mantra.

"Worry about the things you can do something about."

I would come to cherish this phrase and use it as a motivator to let go enough to begin to heal. First, I needed to face my own music. I had to ask myself if the reason my kids were different was truly and actually my fault. Sure, in my case the cause was certain, but was it actually something I *did* to them? None of us can create the traits our kids are born with. Accepting that their lot in life was part of their destiny helped me to let go of feeling so responsible. Some things in life are within our control, and some are not. By framing the experience in this context, I realized that I desperately wanted to be a mom no matter the outcome and couldn't continue to blame myself.

But there was another layer of insight that helped instrumentally. Another line in *Moonstruck*, from Ronny to Loretta, got right to the point: "We aren't here to make things perfect. Snowflakes are perfect. The stars are perfect. Not us. Not us!"

It occurred to me that the best way to not feel guilty about having a child who is different and to forgive myself was to let go of the notion of perfection. As Ronny pointed out, perfection doesn't exist in people. When I started shifting my mindset to the idea that no one is flawless, I began to relinquish the feeling that I'd done something wrong. I even opened myself up to the possibility that just like everyone else, I was blessed to be a parent of a child born exactly as they were meant to be. In fact, I did something absolutely right.

BE HONEST WITH YOURSELF

Are you someone who doesn't care what people think? Or do you tend to be consumed by the thoughts and opinions of others? Be honest with yourself.

I used to think that because I was different, I was the only one absorbed by what others might be thinking of me. But when I was trying to decide whether or not to attend my ten-year high school reunion, I inquired of a friend whether someone I remembered fondly was attending. In fact, she wasn't. My friend explained that our mutual friend had gained weight since graduation and wanted to avoid feeling judged. John and I had just gotten engaged, so I shared what was on my mind with him.

"Seriously? I walk this earth with only one finger on each

hand, shortened arms, and one toe on each foot and she's not coming because she put on a few pounds?"

But that was unfair. Who was I to judge her? Just because my differences were more pronounced didn't negate her own personal struggle. After all, I knew how hard it can be to see yourself in a better light than others do.

After our son Ethan's birth, I couldn't help but stare into his big blue eyes and tiny, sweet face. Although he was breathtakingly beautiful, I was secretly relieved that the nurses had swaddled him tight, with all his limbs covered. It gave me a few moments to fantasize, having a baby who was the vision of perfection for all to see. But then John's parents and mine arrived to meet their grandson. Although it seems so silly given my own physical differences, I longed for them to meet Ethan with his hands and feet covered up. He would appear perfect for their first impression. John had other ideas. Without hesitating, he took our newborn from my arms, and his blanket instantly fell to the ground. Next, he proudly held our son high in the air for our parents to offer their collective oohs and aahs.

"Here he is! *This. Is. Ethan!*"

I was stunned by John's resolute strength. Actually, I shouldn't have been *so* in awe since I had been raised to behave the same way. I remember strolling through a mall with my mom when I was around the age of ten, and a group of tweens passed us. One of them noticed my hands, pointed at me, and snorted out aloud, "Hey, did you see that girl?"

I glanced at my mom and began to pull her to leave. But instead of succumbing to unwelcome attention, she turned and smiled at me.

"Meg, forget them. You look absolutely gorgeous in red. I think I saw a sweater in the Limited you'll love. Come, let's have you try it on!"

She responded to the scene by showing me that while I had no control over others, I always had the power to ignore. As I grew up, both of my parents' commitment in this regard helped me to make the most of my life—I unhesitatingly went on my own to sleepaway camps, joyfully rushed a sorority in college, determinedly moved alone to New York City for law school, and interviewed with confidence afterward, landing competitive jobs on Wall Street and beyond.

But then, when I became a parent of a child who was different, it was as if I had to learn the lesson all over again. My old innate pangs of shame once again reared their ugly heads. I found myself loathing every time a passerby would stare at Ethan in his carriage. Depending on my mood, I'd be at best annoyed and at worst filled with resentment and rage. How dare they look at my child and make us feel less than? But I knew I needed to move past it because their intentions were not harmful, and it wasn't just my own happiness at stake now. I was determined to once again rise to the occasion.

A dear friend who passed away years ago once gave me very important advice: "Meg, don't let anyone take your power away from you."

I felt the depth of her advice. My power was self-love. If I allowed my fears about what other people thought of my family to intrude and overwhelm, my insecurities could crush me, and my kids would lose out, too. So in order for me to be the champion my children deserved, I needed to emulate both my husband and my parents and let go of worrying about what others were thinking so my kids could have the opportunity to thrive.

Once I was fortunate to listen to author and thought leader Caroline Myss, who was being featured on a PBS program in which she said, "The opposite of love is not hate. It's fear."

The sentiment completely resonated. If love is what fulfills us the most, she explained, fear-based decisions always lead us in the wrong direction. I've thought about the interview a lot since I'm quite positive that every misstep I've made as a parent of children who are different was mainly caused by my own fear. Fear of a life I hadn't planned. Fear that I couldn't handle the task placed in front of me. Fear of being pitied. That one is particularly ridiculous given my own personal physique. Sometimes I felt like the only thing I didn't fear was fear itself. But the main fear that I've struggled with the most over the years is the fear of what other people thought of me, and later, my children.

In 1966, Harold Wilson, the prime minister of the United Kingdom, told Queen Elizabeth II, "We can't be everything to everyone and still be true to ourselves."

That advice has served as a guidepost in my own life. Why must I be so caught up with the judgment of others? And the more I try to please them, the farther away I become from being authentically me. And so, I needed to love myself enough to let go of the need to measure myself against the judgment of friends, family, and strangers. Until we achieve self-love, how can we possibly expect it from our kids? It was time to roll up my sleeves because I had important work to do as the mother of a child born different. This reminds me of when you're on an airplane and you hear the in-flight safety briefing telling you to attend to your own oxygen mask before your child's. Before caring for others, you must care for yourself. By focusing on growing your own confidence, you'll teach your children to model that same power.

So, are you like I was and fear people's judgment, or do you truly not care? Be honest with yourself. As a parent of a child who is different, it matters.

LEARNING TO LOVE YOURSELF

How did I do it? How did I love myself enough to stop worrying about what others were thinking about me and my family? Okay, if I'm being honest, I had to fake it at first. When I started my nonprofit, Don't Hide It, Flaunt It, I encouraged everyone to "flaunt," which in this context was code for unconditional self-acceptance.

Next, I thought a lot about advice I'd heard in the context of my day job:

"Confidence is silent. Insecurities are loud."

It dawned on me that in order to demonstrate inner strength in public, I didn't need to do it verbally. I needed to walk the walk. I began posting photos of my one-fingered, shortened arms above my head on social media. I didn't feel ready to go full flaunt but took the initiative anyway. On vacation that year, I braced myself and posted a photo of John and some friends with their ten-toed feet and my one-toed feet dangling next to theirs as we overlooked a gorgeous view of the mountains. That one took tons of extra courage because typically my feet are hidden in my shoes and certainly not posted publicly for people to gawk at.

In forcing myself to flaunt, I was inspired by the teachings of social psychologist and author Amy Cuddy. In her TED Talk, Cuddy described reasons why we need to be aware of our body language and what we're communicating nonverbally: "Your body language shapes who you are."

Cuddy further taught that our posture can affect testosterone and cortisol levels in the brain and change the way we feel about ourselves. That means standing tall and proud, even when we don't feel confident, can have a positive impact on how we're perceived. Essentially, even if we don't say anything, our very physicality can suggest whether we feel uncomfortable. According to Cuddy, "Practice feeling positive and confident. Even if you don't have it in you yet, fake it until you've become it."

Cuddy suggested privately trying a Wonder Woman pose to become more self-assured. I decided to take her advice to the next level, and in my bedroom in front of a mirror, held my hands up high in a V-shape—my own version of her power pose. Of course, not everyone has a blatant difference like mine, but it doesn't matter. These power poses really help mentally prepare you for the inevitable and constant attention you'll experience in public with your child who is different.

Cuddy's teachings really impacted me. One day when Ethan was about three years old, I went for a walk with him while Charlie, then an infant, stayed at home with our nanny. Up until that point, no matter the temperature outside, I'd have brought a light sweater to wear or hold to cover up my arms and hands. But on this occasion, I wore a tank top and left my cover-up at home. Sure, people overtly and discreetly stared at both of us as we walked past the shops in our town. But I made a conscious decision to stop allowing their focus on us to affect my mood. They didn't actually care anything about us, so why should I care about them?

Years after I had first heard Caroline Myss speak, she shared something extremely powerful during an interview with Oprah Winfrey: "Most people are miserable because they're trying to live a life that doesn't belong to them. . . . No one can be truly healthy or fulfilled if their head and their heart exist as two separate forces within them. What you really want . . . is to be madly in love with the life you have."

That sentiment sealed the deal for me. If I can come to accept and even choose to love the life I've been assigned, then why should I possibly care what others might be thinking about me and my children? Embracing this mindset resulted in even greater perks. The more I leaned in to my authentic self, the more magnetic I became to others. And although I couldn't control their reactions, comments, and outbursts, I refused to care.

To my delight, my children have followed my lead. But make no mistake. Once I'd achieved unconditional self-love, it wasn't automatically transferred to them. Just like my parents before me, it would take years of devotion and effort to help them let go of their own fears of external judgment and find their own personal strength and dignity. As their parent, I would experience personal hiccups along the way, sometimes even at their expense. But my efforts began to pay off. Once, when Ethan was ten, I checked in to see if he was anxious about attending a new sleepaway camp. During the conversation, I reminded him that the fact that he looked different was a blessing in disguise.

"E, you won't have to worry about what people think of you. You will attract only the most wonderful kids; they will be the ones who want to know you."

Ethan replied, "Mom, being different is not a blessing in disguise."

"It's not?" Instantly I felt an inner surge of anxiety.

Ethan looked up and smiled.

"Nope, Mom, it's simply a blessing. Why would I care what other people think? You don't."

GIVE YOURSELF A BREAK

A friend whose son has special needs described how scrolling through his own Facebook and Instagram pages became excruciating. No longer was it a quick respite from life's stress. Rather, it felt like torture watching friends near and far happily and effortlessly post photos and updates of their kids leading the life he had expected for his own child, participating in activities he had mistakenly assumed were guaranteed. So every time my friend looked at his computer, he felt numb. Their posts represented things he knew were likely out of reach for his child. He wasn't ready to post and dreaded seeing others' updates.

After sinking further into FOMO while having to face the reality that his son's life wouldn't measure up to what he had planned or match what his friends' kids of the same age were experiencing, he realized the best solution was to take time away from social media. Although it felt a bit drastic at first, he was certain it would give him time to stop worrying about everyone else's milestones and focus on strengthening himself and supporting his family. The pause was without question worthwhile. After some time to heal and renew his perspective, he posted on social media a year later, focusing on how fortunate he was to be sharing his life with his beautiful boy. It's important to take the time you need to process your new normal before sharing it with your extended community. And that's more than okay.

HUMOR HELPS

In the professional world, there is a common expression, "Tone from the top." It means that people will take cues directly from anyone in a leadership position. When you parent a child who is different, you are the leader in this context; it's up to you to not only set the tone for your child but also for strangers. Behavior matters. If you seem unhappy, ashamed, or miserable about your family's lot in life, people will react in kind, often with pity. Or they might simply avoid being around you, or at least avoid talking about anything related to your child's difference. Conversely, if you present yourself as a parent with an aura of positivity and are happy to engage, others can have a different take on what your life is actually like and even long to know you better.

One evening I was walking toward the Port Authority in New York City and noticed a sign with a picture of Ellen DeGeneres. The caption read: "You never know what funny can do."

I caught my breath staring at that message because its truth struck me deeply. The ability to not take everything so seriously and even find the humor in it all is a primary key to helping others feel comfortable. Okay, it doesn't work all the time. I've made jokes about my physical difference, and sometimes it's fallen flat because the person wasn't prepared and clearly felt uncomfortable. But I believe that the encounter, while awkward in the moment, would make them think about it later. Perhaps the next time, they might choose to relax a bit and enjoy someone's self-deprecating chuckle.

I remember one time when another mother sat down next to me on a bench while our children played at a local park. We were talking casually about nothing of importance, but then she noticed Ethan was different. Immediately I picked up on her change in mood, and an awkward silence swallowed our conversation. I am sure she was also worried that her son might say something to Ethan that she would find embarrassing. It was time for me to act.

"Ethan is so happy they finally reopened Castle Park after the renovation that if he could swing it with his one finger, I'm sure he'd pinch himself!"

I purposefully and genuinely laughed, and immediately, the other mother joined in. Again, we began to chat about nothing important. By demonstrating my ability to be lighthearted about my child's difference, I had actually impacted her perspective about us.

KEEP IT IN PERSPECTIVE

When you are focused on your son or daughter who is different, sometimes it can feel as if you're the only one confronted with challenges. It is also easy to get caught up in thinking that everyone must be constantly focused on your child at every encounter. Other parents, however, are often consumed by invisible struggles their own kids are managing. It helps to remind yourself that other people have concerns or fears of their own.

My friend Liz Svatek's story of giving birth to her son Landon underscores this point.

After battling infertility, enduring in vitro, and getting pregnant, I naïvely believed all my troubles were behind me. I had no idea that when my son Landon was born, my life would change forever. I sensed something was wrong. He was a big baby, but toward the end of my pregnancy, I felt like he wasn't moving enough. Thank God for that instinct because it saved his life. I had a nervous feeling as I went to the ER for an emergency C-section at thirty-six weeks. As they struggled to get my epidural to work, his heart rate was dropping. They had a hard time pulling him out, and when they did, there was no sound. They whisked him off to the PICU with my husband trailing behind. I lay on the operating table and cried as they sewed me up.

Landon was born with right arterial thrombosis, a collection of blood clots in his right arm. He'd had a stroke while being delivered via a C-section and could be brain damaged. They said they might need to amputate his right arm because it was causing him such stress. I felt like I was in my own personal hell; I wanted to wall myself away from the world. As I was leaving the hospital days later without a baby, I saw a friend I knew. She was leaving the hospital at the same time with her newborn baby girl. When she asked where Landon was, I almost wanted to lie and say everything was fine. I told her, and she was sympathetic, but I felt sick. I didn't want her or anyone else's pity. On the way home, I felt myself detaching. I was so afraid Landon would die that I was pretending he had never been born. People were reaching out, but it was hard to let them in. People started dropping off beautiful dinners and cards and calling. I felt my heart opening, I needed support, I started accepting help and feeling less alone. Landon remained in the hospital but started getting better. His brain was unaffected, he opened his eyes, his arm was stable.

After fifty-two days, he could now go home. Although I'd wished that he could come home for so long, I was now terrified. I was going home with a newborn with a bloody and scarred-up right arm. What would Landon's life be like? Would people be scared of him? Landon's right arm and hand were noticeably different. I started thinking about all the staring, mean comments, and rude glances he would have to endure his whole life, and my heart felt heavy. I felt myself hiding, staying small, just hanging around my house and neighborhood where we were safe. I allowed close friends to come over. They reassured me with their happy reactions, their hopeful looks, our shared tears. Landon was home, he was safe, he was going to be okay. I pushed through my fears and started taking him out publicly. I loved to dress him up in fancy clothes, little embroidered Jon-Jons with depictions of frogs or cars, little preppy kid clothes.

There were some stares. I just tried to ignore them. I will never forget one of the first people to approach me in a restaurant. She had been staring for a long time. When she started to approach, I sat up straight as an arrow ready for battle. She came up to my table and said, "I love that embroidered outfit! Where'd you get it? She is such a pretty baby!" No comment on his arm, and she thought he was so "pretty" that he was a girl! I was floored. I realized I couldn't control how people reacted to Landon, but I also didn't want to assume every interaction would be a negative one.

After that, I tried not to hide Landon's arm in long sleeves or jackets unless the temperature warranted it. I went to Mommy and Me classes, lunches and dinners, and outings in the park, and most of the time, no one said a word about his arm. When they did, I tried to be patient and offer simple explanations. Most of the parents were lovely. They were friendly, asking about nap times and normal development milestones. I realized that the more I was okay with Landon, the more everyone else was, too.

When it was time to send Landon to preschool, I was so emotional, so terrified, but I tried to hide it from Landon. Would kids make fun of him? Shun him? I watched as Landon went to class and started playing with the kids. There were a couple of looks, one kid even touched Landon's arm, but then Landon smiled and they both moved on. Wait, that was it? I had tears in my eyes as the teacher approached me. I told her my fears. She looked at me, smiling. "All parents feel this way. I find it's much more upsetting to them than to the kids." I looked around at all the other teary parents. We were all scared, letting go, trusting that our kids could handle this next important step of independence. We were all hoping that our kids would fit in, be lovingly accepted for who they were despite visible or invisible differences.

KEEPING YOUR SAFE PEOPLE CLOSE

When you have a baby or child who becomes different, people with the best of intentions may feel like they have a special license to ask probing questions, weigh in, or get all the answers right away. It can feel like a fast-speeding train coming right at you. The experience reminds me of getting engaged, sharing the exciting news, and instantly being barraged with questions before I had all the answers, like: Have you set the date yet? Am I your maid of honor? Where's the wedding going to be? Will it be big or small? Can we invite Aunt Sadie?

They mean well, of course. And yet, it's simply too soon to

satisfy their need to know more. Unlike the happy occasion of a wedding celebration, though, the experience of having a child who is different is not one you're inclined to celebrate, at least not yet. It's best to remind people who are prematurely poking that you just need time to process things. If they care about you, they will understand. And if not, it's not your problem. You have more important things to focus on.

Keep the safe people in your life close. Whether family members or friends, safe people don't press before you're ready. They never judge you and instinctively follow your lead. With them, we can cry in self-pity one minute, and then the next moment, laugh so hard, we cry again. We cherish our safe people because they give us the chance to be our authentic selves. They also may act as a defensive tackle when others prematurely press for more information about our baby's or child's condition.

When Ethan was a baby and someone would stare at his hands, I'd pretend they had the face of Lia, a best friend from college and one of my safest people. For me, it was another form of Cuddy's "fake it until you become it" because it created a visual zone of comfort until I felt mentally strong enough to deal with the ongoing and unwelcome attention. It works. During those early years, I desperately leaned on my safe people, who continually reminded me that only the people who matter, well . . . matter.

My dad describes calling his older brother Dave on the day I was born. At the time, my parents lived in Illinois, a thousand miles from my relatives in New York. Even after my dad tried to describe my condition over the phone, Dave didn't quite get it. Out of love and concern, Dave understandably kept asking him questions. But as my father was trying to figure everything out himself, he wasn't fully prepared to respond. It's also really hard to read someone over the phone. Had my uncle been local, I'm quite positive he would've been one of my father's safe people. In other words, don't dismiss a person as unsafe simply because they don't immediately understand your needs.

SHARING THE NEWS AT WORK

An acquaintance once told me that after her son received an unexpected diagnosis while she was still on maternity leave, she quickly realized that her new normal also meant having to balance it all with her professional life. Since she'd need to arrive to work late or leave early on occasion for an appointment, the mere thought of returning to work with her new priorities at home triggered immense anxiety.

On her first day back, her colleagues enthusiastically welcomed her with heartfelt congratulations. They also blurted out things like:

- "How's he doing?"

- "Has he said his first word yet?"

- "What's his latest milestone?"

- "It may seem hard now, but don't worry, it gets easier."

Despite the well-meaning questions and comments, she struggled, reluctant to share any candid details. Although her baby boy was her bundle of joy, his challenges by extension were now hers. These questions were typical but still caught her off guard.

In the end, while you might owe it to someone at work to explain potential irregularities in your schedule, deciding whether to go into detail about your family's particular circumstances is a personal choice. Don't feel the need to overshare as if everyone is deserving. Someone who seemingly cares but is ultimately being nosy isn't entitled to hear your business on any topic anyway. But it can help to have at least one person at work in whom you can confide. Just remember that the colleague who was genuine, trustworthy, and loyal before you left to have your baby or learned of a new diagnosis is the same person who will know intuitively just how to support you while following your lead. In that sense, the concept of keeping your safe people close also extends to your work life.

MANAGING THE WELL-MEANING ENCOUNTERS

Dr. Adrienne Scott, a researcher at Johns Hopkins University, conducted a poll that asked participants the following question: "What do people fear the most?" Blindness came in first, which was ranked overall equal to or worse than losing a limb or hearing, even getting cancer. In a nutshell, participants in the survey were more afraid of being different than getting a life-threatening disease.

It makes me think about the best-selling pregnancy/baby bible, *What to Expect When You're Expecting* by Heidi Murkoff, which has been around for decades and is filled with practical tips, empathetic wisdom, key strategies, and lifestyle choices designed to guide you throughout your pregnancy. But as useful as it may be, I've noticed people recommend skipping over certain sections. Why? Because it also covers things that could possibly go wrong. I've come to believe that if you spend time with people who think your life represents what went wrong, it's only natural for them to behave as they are (likely) thinking, "I am glad it wasn't me." Their typical impulse, therefore, is to jump into action to help make you feel better. Or they simply don't know what to say. Or they are afraid of their children encountering your children and doing the wrong thing. One particular incident comes to mind. Another nursery school mother whose son was Ethan's age, two years old at the time, approached me after we had just moved to the area.

"Excuse me, what am I supposed to tell my child about your son? He's never seen anything like him."

To her, the question was perfectly reasonable. To me, it felt uncomfortably probing and intrusive. I was speechless (a rarity for me). Appearing miffed, she turned and walked away. That evening, after I read Ethan a book and put him and his baby brother, Charlie, to bed, I followed my husband, John, into our bedroom. I couldn't contain my anger and resentment.

"What the hell?! Who does that rude woman think she is? Why does she think she can ask me a question like that?"

It's a good thing I hadn't yet heard how weeks earlier the same mother, after learning about Ethan's condition and anticipating his arrival, had begged the school to make different arrangements. If Ethan *had* to attend, she petitioned, it would be better for everyone if he were placed in a separate classroom with a special ed teacher. This way his needs, whatever she assumed they were, wouldn't supersede the regular routine of the other students.

When Ethan was a baby, we lived in Larchmont, New York. One particularly hot summer day, I took him for a walk in his stroller. Not in the mood for anyone to stare at him, I initially covered him with a light blanket up to his neck. But after a few blocks, I could see Ethan was getting uncomfortable from the heat, so I had no choice but to remove it. He was only wearing a light blue onesie. Suddenly, a woman I'd never met passed us, peered into Ethan's stroller, and stopped to offer her unsolicited thoughts.

"Oh, honey. It's okay. Is he only your first? You're still young. There are wonderful special needs programs in the schools here. Don't worry!"

I was extremely put off that she felt she had the license to weigh in with whatever was on her mind. As she waved goodbye, I couldn't help but wonder—had she noticed my own limb difference too? I wasn't certain since I had covered up my own arms and hands with a sweater. When I told John that evening what had happened, he responded directly.

"Get used to it."

He wasn't kidding. Other parents have also told me about strangers approaching them, seeing their baby, and literally saying aloud, "Geez. You are taking it so well. If it was me, I don't think I could handle it."

If I had paid closer attention throughout my childhood, I'd have noticed how many times my parents had to endure unwelcome reactions and outbursts from strangers. Until I became *that* parent too, it never occurred to me that I wasn't the only one having to manage the experience. Recently I asked my mom how she felt when so many strangers thrust comments about me in her direction. Her answer reminded me how my parents and husband are cut from the same cloth.

"Of course I was frustrated, Meg, especially with some of the insensitive comments. It was difficult to repress my own anger, but I did. Deep in my heart I knew I couldn't control others, only myself. It was much more important to teach that lesson to you than waste my energy reacting to them."

For a parent of a child who is different, it is extremely useful to know in advance what to anticipate. Not only can it take off the edge in the moment, but it can even lead to a private chuckle at home afterward. And to be fair, many people you encounter are simply struggling with how best to manage an unexpected meeting with your family and want to do or say the right thing but just don't know how. It's complicated. That said, I have found that their reactions, even with the best of intentions, invariably fall into the following categories:

- **The Pitiers:** When they encounter you and your child, they offer a long and consoling look. They may also let out an audible "Tsk, tsk, tsk."

- **The Physicians:** Without a medical degree or license, they can't wait to authoritatively provide groundless advice about your child's condition and what to expect. Oh, and their bedside manner is often terrible.

- **The Fortune-Tellers:** They don't know what to say, so instead blurt out, "I am sure everything will be just fine." If they are of an older generation, they might add the word "dear" at the end of that sentence.

- **The "I Know"ers:** They try to comfort you by telling you that their sister's husband's second cousin's child had the same condition and *they* turned out fine. Or they attempt to reassure you, "I know of someone whose kid has 'it' too. But don't worry, you'll get through this!"

- **The Helpers:** They don't know what to say, so they offer, "Is there anything I can do to help you get through this?" They might even want to send a platter. It does not go unnoticed that the same is often offered when a relative dies.

- **The Texters:** They may be a distant friend who isn't willing to really be there for you. So, rather than reaching out directly in person or by calling, they just send you a text letting you know they're here if you need them. They might even add a caring emoji at the end of their message.

- **The Side-Glancers:** They pretend not to notice that your child is different but can't stop themselves from giving a side-glance stare. It can feel just as intrusive as if they'd gawked directly.

- **The Curious Cats:** They bombard you with questions about your child to keep the conversation going, although you might not even be able to answer many of those questions yourself.

- The Bunglers (Type I): They don't know about your child's difference until they see you with your child and blurt out an audible "Oh!" or similarly awkward reaction. Embarrassed, they apologize for the outburst.

- The Bunglers (Type II): They notice your child's difference and say something inappropriate or insensitive. They might even walk away and feel self-congratulatory that they got through the difficult moment, believing their words offered comfort or help. Instead, you left the encounter deflated and vulnerable.

- The Distractors: They have no idea what to say, so they purposefully talk to you about everything *but* your child's difference. They are likely being polite, but if you have a close relationship with them, you might resent them or feel disappointed that they didn't check in directly.

- The Silent Types: They don't say anything, leaving you wondering if they noticed or know about your child's difference. They could be strangers or people at your office. They are also likely trying to be polite.

Intuitively, people close to you usually know the very thing to do or say the first time they meet your baby—but that is an unrealistic expectation for strangers. Even with the best of intentions, their myriad reactions can feel annoying and even intrusive. When Ethan was a baby, motivated to enlighten and longing to vent, I shared examples of my experience with a good friend. Always direct, she put me on the spot.

"Well, Meg, how *should* people react when encountering you with Ethan?"

The question was fair and deserved an answer. I explained to her that all I wanted was for people to treat us like they'd treat anyone else. If you're close to me, then be there for me. And if you aren't, then tell me how adorable my child is—it's certainly something every parent loves to hear. And if that isn't genuine, then the "Silent Type" works too.

Sometimes I wish I could go back in time to the morning that the other mother at Ethan's nursery school nervously approached me. I was so resentful and angry at her. But the reality was that her actions (to my face and otherwise) were not intentionally harmful. Rather, they were triggered by something I shared at the time—fear. Who am I to judge her for that? Perhaps I could've even defused her own anxiety. It seems so obvious to me now how I might have responded when she asked for advice about how to speak to her son about Ethan's difference:

"Umm . . . don't bother mentioning it? He will figure it out on his own, I'm quite sure." Or, "If he continues to ask, just be matter-of-fact and truthful. Maybe they can even become friends."

By not responding that morning so many years ago, I missed an opportunity.

WHEN LIFE DOESN'T GO ACCORDING TO PLAN

Consider the things in our lives that were unexpected but turned out to be equally if not more beautiful. Buckle up for a wild ride because having a child who is different can be more glorious and rewarding than you anticipated. But first you need to allow yourself to let go of what might have been as if it were the only road to happiness. It is, after all, possible to treasure the family life you hadn't planned. I can't help but think of a couple I read about whose wedding was profiled one Sunday in the *New York Times*. Born with cerebral palsy, Nick Cugini was marrying the love of his life and fellow Yale debate team member, Stacey Chen. But what impressed me the most was what Nick's mother said about her son.

"We didn't know [Nick] was going to be born with a disability. And when we realized it, we just shifted gears and said, 'OK, whatever his dreams are, whatever he wants to accomplish, we are going to make that happen.'"

All kids who are different deserve parents who can pivot with that unfaltering resolve.

Back when my mother was pregnant with me in Urbana, Illinois, there were no scans to provide insight into any expected abnormalities. My physical difference was the last thing my parents expected. Even the doctors and nurses were so unfamiliar with my condition that none could offer a medical term for it. While my mom slept, exhausted both emotionally and physically, the night I was born, my father was still in shock and dragged himself through the snow to his car in the parking lot and sat by himself and wept. Recently, he described the scene to me.

"I don't cry easily, but I was terrified for your future."

"How long did you cry?" I asked him.

"Not for long," he responded. "As a parent with a baby born so blatantly different, and when few things were certain, I didn't have the luxury for my anxiety to be prolonged. Your mom and I . . . we had to rise to the occasion. Everything we thought we understood about our lives and being parents went out the window. But, Meg, you made it easier for us. To our delight, it was hard to be caught up with your hands and feet since you were in many respects, hypernormal. Delightfully happy and naturally positive, you also had more energy than anyone we'd ever met. Early on, we figured out we needed to follow your lead rather than vice versa. That's when I knew everything would be okay. It eventually occurred to me that these were the real cards we'd both been dealt."

As he spoke, I began to reflect. The depth of what my parents had willingly undertaken had never occurred to me. While my arrival shook them to their core and brought them into a new dimension they hadn't anticipated, their choice to get pregnant again with my younger brother, Ted, was not insignificant. It symbolized both my parents' complete acceptance of me and how they had come to understand that the unexpected journey could be one they'd be willing to make all over again. Similarly, my husband and I decided to get pregnant again with Charlie a couple of years after Ethan was born. I was no longer in denial but fully aware of the risks of once again passing along my condition. By this time, Ethan was thriving, however, and we knew we were excited to have another child regardless of the outcome.

Mark Mahaney, a father of a son born with Down syndrome and autism, refers to the perfect analogy that I've used time and time again when describing how raising kids who are different becomes an unexpected gift.

The tests administered during pregnancy for Down syndrome and other conditions somehow didn't indicate Down—so, yes, Noah's condition was certainly a surprise. Frankly, for the first twenty-four hours of Noah's life, his condition was a dramatically negative surprise to me and to my wife. Neither of us was prepared for the news. For me, there was a temporary sadness in thinking about all the experiences that I assumed Noah wouldn't be able to enjoy or fully appreciate during his life.

My first reaction was to order every book on Down syndrome that I could find on Amazon. Busy-ness and focus allowed me to deal with the sadness. But what really got me moving on and fully embracing Noah in a very short time frame was a conversation with a dear friend. When I expressed my sadness about all the life experiences Noah would be missing out on, he gently asked me whether that sadness was based on my expectations for Noah or on Noah's eventual experiences. His point was that Noah could very well have a happy, full life (on his terms, rather than my expectations), and that perhaps that was something to appreciate and possibly celebrate. That conversation helped prepare me to fully accept and embrace Noah.

There's an article that I think is given to many parents when their children are born with disabilities. It's called "Welcome to Holland" and was written by Emily Perl Kingsley. The analogy goes like this: A family plans a full, fun vacation to Italy, but the plane gets diverted and they end up in Holland. The point is that while an unexpected trip to Holland is not the same as a trip to Italy, it still has its charms—windmills, dikes, wooden shoes, and more.

Since having Noah, I've thought about that article many times over the years. And I've thought about how I'd retitle and rewrite it. I think I'd go with the title: "Welcome to Life." Having Noah has been a blessing. And a blessing. And a blessing. Did I plan for Noah? No. But neither did I plan for the three other boys who became his brothers. And they are all wonderful, challenging, delightful, puzzling, loving, patience-testing, and inspiring in their own ways.

FINDING YOUR (NEW) COMMUNITY

Sometimes I'd meet moms who would invite me to join their Mommy and Me parenting group. To be honest, it can feel pretty isolating when other parents are chatting about things that are out of reach for your own child. It's like being part of a book club where everyone is excitedly talking about a book discussing the advantages of living in the United Kingdom when you live in Slovakia. Feel free to join in if you want, but it's also okay to pass in favor of finding people who can better empathize with your family's journey. Or, if it gives you comfort to spend time with friends who've had babies the same age, maybe give both types of parenting circles a shot. Mostly, pay attention to where you feel the most relaxed.

While raising our sons, I made a huge mistake. When Ethan was a little boy and Charlie a toddler, a friend mentioned to me that there was a foundation whose mission was to introduce limb-different children to each other so that they could feel like part of a larger community where they had something in common. I recall feeling instantly offended and complaining to John, "Why would the boys need to meet other children that look like them? They have each other, and me for that matter!"

Yeah, I realize I was being short-sighted. And probably a bit self-hating. I think the younger me who had spent years trying to assimilate was kicking in, unable to fathom the idea of my kids being lumped into a category of people who were different. The following year, the same organization invited me to be one of their keynote speakers and to bring our family to their weekend-long annual event filled with activities for the children. At first, I hesitated. Would this be a good idea? I had to stop and recognize my hypocrisy. There I was, regularly speaking as an advocate for celebrating difference before any group that would invite me, yet now I was contemplating avoiding a limb-difference organization's event. Yikes! What was I thinking? So, I agreed to present there, and it was wonderful. At that point, I had been writing about my own life experience on a blog, but after I spoke, several kids ran up to me and asked if they could write about their stories and accomplishments. One kid had just learned to play the drums with only one hand. Another loved to dance despite having differently formed feet. This would be the

spark that gave me insight into how important it was to empower the voices of kids who looked or felt different.

Yet, even then, I wasn't fully embracing the event. Rather
than giving my kids the opportunity to spend the maximum
amount of time with the other kids at the conference, we left
shortly after my speech and went to Boston to go sightseeing.
I think I still had to process what I had seen at that meeting
and what role I wanted to play going forward.

When we got home, I took a conscious break and began
listening to many other parents of kids with a host of differences and disabilities. They talked about the importance of
finding their new community of fellow parents whose children
shared the same condition. They also shared how much it
meant to their children to become friends with other children
who shared their life experiences, even if it was only as pen pals
or long-distance friends who talked on the phone until they
could reunite at the same foundation event each year.

For example, Michelle Veloso's daughter, Sydney, was diagnosed with type 1 diabetes at age ten. Although she appeared
physically perfect, Sydney felt the opposite. Michelle watched
as Sydney became extremely self-conscious. Sydney begged her
mom not to tell anyone. Weary and stressed in her own right,
Michelle realized she needed to help Sydney move forward.
Instead of sending her to the sleepaway camp she had been
scheduled to attend, Michelle found a camp for Sydney that
was just for kids with diabetes. When Sydney returned home
from camp, the transformation was obvious. She no longer felt
self-conscious—she even chose to wear her insulin pump ex-
ternally, unafraid of the inevitable attention from her peers at

school. Simply *telling* Sydney that there were other kids going through the same thing was insufficient, but *spending time* with those kids gave her back her dignity.

Hearing these stories reminded me that as a child, I too would long to see anyone who looked different, like me. I recalled many past Fourth of July celebrations where I was immersed in a crowd of strangers who were looking up at the fireworks. I, on the other hand, would be scanning the field, hoping to catch a glimpse of some fellow limb-different kid. But whether or not I realized it at the time, I think what I was truly longing for was to actually know and talk to someone who looked like me, not just know they existed. And so, after hearing from Michelle and other parents, I started to regret keeping our boys isolated in a cocoon of kids who didn't share their life experience.

Recently, I asked Ethan if he felt like he had missed out by not spending more time with people who shared our condition or something similar. His response was telling: "I guess I never felt like I was missing anything at the time. But actually, Mom, it makes me wonder what it would have been like to have a friend born like me. I'm definitely still curious."

THE UNEXPECTED GIFT

Years ago, when I first started writing about my experience as a mother of sons who share my condition, I began to receive many e-mails from parents new to the experience of having a child who was different. For them, thoughts of the road ahead felt daunting; many wanted to know how I was able to be so positive.

The first time I ever entertained the idea that there might be an upside to my condition was when I was a teenager. One evening, I sat on my bed, sobbing to my father. My first boyfriend had just broken up with me, and I was completely devastated. I was convinced that no one would ever want to marry me, given my physical traits. My father looked at me and spoke reassuringly.

"Meg, I can't predict the timing, but the person who will want to commit to you will be the most special, biggest-hearted, un-superficial person."

His words would come true, but not only with respect to the man I married. They also applied to all the people who chose to have relationships with me, platonic or otherwise. In effect, I've weeded out the superficial jerks in life just by being me. As I grew older, I began to realize there were even more perks. Despite all the people staring at me, so many others offer me a smile for no reason at all. It happens a lot. I once asked my brother Peter if people reacted in the same way when he entered a room. He had no idea what I was talking about. I've also taken numerous taxi rides where the driver waves me off when I try to pay. And long lines at the airport? At one glance, the majority of security folks usher me and our family to the front of the security line. I used to resent it, feeling as if we were being pitied or granted unfair favoritism. Maybe we were. But it took me years to finally learn to swallow my pride and enjoy receiving kindness for kindness's sake. Just today, I swung by a Starbucks to get a grande latte, and the barista handed me a venti. Knowing I had paid for the smaller size, I let her know she had made a mistake. She looked at me warmly. "Yes, I know. Have a great day. Enjoy it."

In the blog I used to write, periodically I would share various iterations of my "Top Ten Reasons It's Amazing to Have Two Fingers." Here are some of my favorites:

- You don't need the name tag at the reunion. They'll all remember you.

- Callbacks on interviews are a given. Let's face it—they want to know more.

- The Apple Store employee will take you as a walk-in, even when there are no appointments available.

- When you raise your hand in class, you almost always get picked first.

- If someone needs extra help with manual labor, you are the last person they'll call.

- When you're growing up, your teachers will take an instant shine to you.

- Almost everything you do, even shoveling snow, strikes people as incredible.

It was fun to brainstorm that list, but it never occurred to me until I became a parent of children who are different that there was even more to gain. For example, I've realized that being petty about things is a waste of time. I am also sensitive to not judge others, knowing how it feels to be judged. I no longer sweat the small stuff; I am actually grateful for the little things in life. I've broadened my contacts to an amazing community of people I would've never otherwise met. I am more willing to be adaptable. My sincerity is a given. I'm not competitive with other parents, just content with my own children's accomplishments. I've gained a deeper understanding of what's truly important. I've also discovered it's pointless to try to control everything all the time. While none of us had envisioned or desired having a child who is different, the truth is that we've been blessed.

I ask myself now, what was I so afraid of? Failing my children? Failing myself? It occurs to me that with many children, parents' expectations are automatically high from the start. But as some of those aspirations go, inevitably unmet, the goal is to release disappointment (yours and theirs) and help everyone embrace reality. But when you're a parent of a child who is different, you've let go of standard expectations from the very beginning. As a result, every step your child takes toward independence and self-development becomes a joyful and rewarding leap for you both.

Not only can you be the parent who is poised to empower your child, but that same kid becomes directly responsible for your own unforeseen growth. Conquering your biggest fears and embracing your new normal becomes the greatest of gifts.

CHAPTER 2

Building Your Child's Dignity

While many parents of kids who are born different are understandably focused on their children's physical abilities, supporting kids emotionally is equally, if not even more, important. We desperately want our kids to be content, secure, and ideally as carefree as their peers. But when you live your life as if you're a car wreck on the side of the road while the entire world is rubbernecking to get a good gawk, the unwelcome attention can wear even the toughest person down. Because it's all the more challenging to keep positive, helping to build your child's sense of self is essential. While therapists may be helpful depending on your child's age, you play the most important role in building your children's dignity. This critical work needs to be accomplished mainly at home, behind the scenes. It's like teaching a kid how to tread water. Above the surface, they learn to keep their head up and remain calm, but beneath is where all the effort is made.

Someone once told me that we need to raise our kids empathetically, so they feel like we're telling them, "I get you." Some parents take this to the nth degree. I once read a CBS News article about a dad who spent thirty hours getting a massive tattoo across his torso to match the birthmark of his eight-year-old son. Knowing his son was very self-conscious, this dad was desperate for him to be able to go swimming and feel happy, comfortable, and not alone in his experience. "I knew he was self-conscious about it. I saw how he was reacting, and it made me want to do it so that he wouldn't be the only one." This father wanted his son to know that he could lean on him when times got tough. Whatever steps we take to support our children, however, they must come to realize that we won't always be there to catch every emotional fall. Therefore, it's our job to help them build their self-worth. It's not because we don't want to be there for them, but simply because we can't always be there.

Growing up, I often hid my hands in my pockets. What other people thought about me certainly mattered. Yet the only people who actually mattered accepted me for me. Living as a "hider" during my youth has prompted me to think a lot about the topic of shame, not to be confused with feeling ashamed. We likely heard the latter when we were young and being reprimanded: "You should be ashamed of yourself!"

Feeling ashamed is brought on by something we did wrong, like getting caught in a white lie. Shame, however, can be triggered by something out of our control, like when your child receives unwelcome attention because of their difference.

As their advocate, you must strengthen your son or daughter to the point where they are not influenced by a judgmental gaze or insensitive outburst hurled in their direction. It is up to you, therefore, to help them secure a safe landing when there's no escaping the reality of all the unwelcome attention. And the fact that the other person meant well or was simply curious doesn't mean it feels any better on the receiving end. Fortunately, when you help your child establish their dignity, they will be prepared to rise to the occasion.

CURIOSITY IS NORMAL

As soon as your child is old enough to notice other kids focusing on them (and it can be the worst part of their day), the time is ripe to help them understand that fascination or even fear about their difference should be anticipated.

Help your child gain deeper insight into what makes someone curious. Describe entering a park and all of a sudden seeing something unexpected, like a yellow frog, a purple sky, or a bright orange mouse. Ask your child to be honest with you about what they would do in that situation. Would *they* run to the slide or monkey bars, or instead stare at the unexpected object? Explain it so they understand that the reaction from the other child is actually quite normal. Inquiring minds want to know!

Consider involving them in an art project where they can create something unique but also beautiful. An Internet search can also be useful to inspire them. For my own kids, I did a search on peacocks and found images of them with average and also unexpected colors. We agreed that the atypical white-bodied peacock was the most beautiful of them all. These efforts will help your child understand how other kids are experiencing something new when they meet them, while still reminding your child that different doesn't have to mean worse than the norm.

One morning when Charlie was six and his younger sister, Savanna, was five, I took them to their favorite local playground, Castle Park. Always on the monkey bars, Savanna instantly made a friend. When Savanna noticed Charlie on the slide, she and her new pal ran over to join him. At first the three of them were giggling and delighted as they kept climbing to the top of the stairs and coming down the slide. Then Savanna decided they should try walking up the plastic slide. Charlie followed his sister's method and used each of his two-fingered hands to grasp the sides of the slide as he jutted himself upward. He was older than the girls and actually the fastest up. Savanna's new friend began pointing at Charlie.

"Ewwww! What happened to your hands? How can you go up that slide if you don't have ten fingers?"

This drew the attention of other kids, who stared at him. I asked John to remain with Savanna as Charlie ran away. I overheard her explaining, "My brother has better handwriting than you do and . . ."

Though the girl's outburst had been innocent, it had stung Charlie—and me, quite frankly. I decided to wait until later to talk about it further, however. Charlie needed space and time to emotionally process the encounter.

In the evening, after reading a book together, I asked Charlie to pretend he was the little girl from the park, while I pretended to be him. At first, he didn't want to participate, but I persisted, so he shouted at me, "Ewww! Look at your hands. Gross!"

I noticed he had added the word "gross"—something she hadn't actually said. It reminded me that our perception can feel far more painful than what was intended.

I responded, "I was just born this way." And then I added, "Hey, I like how fast you ran up that slide. Let's race!"

I then asked what he would do if the same girl had something he'd never seen, like neon-yellow eyes. Would he react in a similar way? Charlie accepted that he might, so I continued, "Charlie, there might be difficult kids you're just going to have to deal with, but don't forget, curious kids are not trying to be mean even though it makes you feel bad inside. They are just surprised. Hey, they might even assume that being different means we are less capable. Imagine being on a racetrack, and the other racers might not think we are supposed to be at the same starting line as them. They can even feel threatened if they see you doing better than them. Don't tell them you're one of them—show them."

His expression became much calmer, so I added, "Of course, if they can't move on, you can leave."

Charlie needed to know that he didn't have to endure anything beyond his own comfort zone, even when another kid's behavior was simply rooted in curiosity and assumptions. But it was my duty to help him anticipate every angle. Whether it was fair or not, both our boys would come to realize that they needed to mature more quickly than their peers. Mostly, it was in their best interest to understand that curiosity was normal.

KEEPING IT HONEST

Early on, as your child begins to notice they are unique, they will come to you wanting answers. Other young kids will question your child, and your child will bring those questions to you first. They will long to be like everyone else. And they'll want you to explain why they're different, often repeatedly. After all, they need to feel prepared. If only you could act on your desire to tell them what they (and you) wish to hear:

- "It's okay, hon. This is temporary."

- "They're just staring at you since you are so beautiful."

- "Kids won't always stare."

- "You'll see. This won't always be so hard."

Nevertheless, the more straightforward and factual you can be early on, the better. In short, although you'll wish to put rose-colored glasses on your child to keep them content and feeling secure in the moment, they deserve a parent who tells it like it is, helping them learn to accept the way things are. I know this may sound harsh, especially when they're very young. The reality, however, is that our kids who are different are forced to develop emotional maturity much sooner than their peers. By responding honestly to their curiosity and circumstances, you avoid setting them up for unrealistic expectations and disappointment later. My mother shared a journal entry from when I was four that underscores the importance of this.

Meg is a child of extreme sensibility. Perceptive and intelligent, she notices the slightest changes in her environment. If I am wearing a new pair of shoes, or even a different colored lipstick, she's the first to comment. Usually in the form of asking "why?" I shall be surprised if she does not show ability in art. This morning, while we were slicing and freezing mushrooms, she asked why the tinfoil was different colors when you folded it. What she saw reflected in the silver paper was her own yellow shirt and my red one; I had never noticed tinfoil reflections.

It is clear, even at this early stage, that she will always want to have five fingers on each hand. She first became aware of her physical difference at age two and a half, and even more so at age three, when she entered a fairly verbal nursery school class. The kids questioned her, and she questioned us. We told her that she had one finger because she was born with one finger. Meg seemed to accept it. But then there was the day she started whining in frustration that she wanted five fingers. I told her that people can't always get what they want, and she stopped.

If she can't do something, she assumes she'll be able to do it when she's older, an assumption that is probably correct. She walked when she was eighteen months old. She learned to take off her shoes when she was three. At four, she still can't tie them, but neither can her brother Peter, who is five. She never had any trouble holding a spoon or a pen. She has excellent control, probably because in addition to wrapping her finger around an object, she has an extra joint in her wrist, which she rests it on. We have been lucky this way. She finds ways of doing most things herself. She climbs slides, has no trouble holding on to swings—she wraps much of her lower arm around the chains.

Above all, she is supremely self-confident, open, joyous, loving, and spontaneous. However, the fact that she is born different has not always been easy for her to accept. She is still wearing size 4 baby shoes, and even those are still too big for her feet. Her feet are now about the same length as that of my eight-month-old son. At first, I told her that when she was bigger, she could wear bigger shoes. But that was a mistake. You can't fool her. She knows she's big enough now. The truth is always simplest. I told her she has to have shoes that fit her feet, and she accepted that.

Meg shows a remarkable ability to dismiss the negative and concentrate on the positive. I saw her sitting by herself in the living room with a thoughtful expression on her face. When I asked her what she was doing, she replied that she was thinking about something, and joyfully sprang to her feet and ran to meet her friends and brother. Of course, I do not know whether she was thinking of her difference, but some reflection on it was quite natural. Her spirit is strong, open, joyous, and beautiful.

TAKE CONTROL OF WHAT YOU CAN AND RELEASE WHAT YOU CAN'T

Many years ago, a friend asked over drinks what I would wish for if I had a genie in a bottle. That's easy, I told her. If only I could control the thoughts and behavior of others. I think the first time I thought of this wish was as a teenager trying to use mental telepathy to force my crush to call. Instead, I stared at my red Princess phone for hours. But as a parent of children who are different, this wish was magnified to an extreme; it would have rescued me from the terrible angst of witnessing my kids feel uncomfortable when other kids approached and started asking questions.

Having this wish granted was impossible, however. And anyway, it wasn't actually what my kids or I truly needed. Our sons have developed an inner strength that I know from personal experience means they'll be prepared for anything into adulthood. Just the other day, while I was sitting outside a coffee shop, a stranger approached me. He explained that if I joined his church, I would be blessed, and my fingers would suddenly "grow back in." Apparently, according to him, it happened to a baby missing feet thousands of years ago and he saw no reason why it couldn't happen for me, too. Sure, he was riding the crazy train, but I thanked him for thinking of me. Most notably, instead of being annoyed or taking offense, I easily rolled with it after years of practice.

A week before Charlie was headed off to his first day of kindergarten, we stopped at a local park near our house.

"Imagine you're at a playground and another boy is swinging back and forth. Can you stop him from swinging just by staring at him?"

Charlie shook his head.

"Okay, now imagine you're on the swing, going higher and higher. Okay, now can you stop?"

Charlie nodded his head in the affirmative.

"Charlie, when kids say things to you, stare at you, or ask you the same question about your hands over and over, you're not going to be able to stop them. It's like they're swinging."

He looked at me deflated. My mind raced to my own childhood, remembering how distraction was the key to taking control of a conversation, even when I couldn't change someone else's reaction to my difference. Every time I was asked why I had only one finger, I'd rush to answer with a quick "I was born this way" and ask them about themselves. Or, my favorite go-to approach was to choose something—anything—about them and offer a sincere compliment. Flattery and mutual interest would distract and help them move on.

So I told my son, "But wait, Char! Remember, you have the power over your own swing. You can sway how the conversation will go. You can tell them you were born this way. You can ask them questions about themselves. You can even walk away if you're not getting anywhere. You can make any of that happen."

Now that my sons are older, I love knowing that they wouldn't share the same wish I once had if a genie came knocking. They accept the fact that they can only control themselves, which is its own power. As my father says, "Worry about the things you can do something about." It is essential to teach your child that it is pointless to focus on things that are out of their control since they cannot change anyone's behavior or reactions, only their own. Having that mindset, they are empowered to go with the flow in a host of situations and be the strongest version of themselves.

Donna Agostino is a devoted mother of three, including a beautiful daughter named Victoria who has alopecia, a condition that causes hair loss. One summer, Victoria told her mom she wanted to put her hair in two braids. Because her condition mainly impacts the back of her head, the desired hairstyle dramatically revealed Victoria's condition. Inwardly, Donna could feel her stomach drop, concerned her daughter would be the subject of unwelcome attention the minute she left the house. Adjusting to a physical difference that comes later in your child's life can be particularly difficult for everyone. It took everything in Donna's power not to speak her mind and say, "Don't do it. People will stare!"

Instead, she turned to Victoria and said, "Oh, your hair looks so pretty. Look in the mirror at the back of your head to make sure you're ready."

Victoria looked at her reflection momentarily, then proudly showed off her braids.

"Mom, I don't care. I want to go out and look this way."

Donna was floored and thrilled by Victoria's strength and commitment to taking control of the wheel on her otherwise unanticipated journey.

More recently, Donna shared that Victoria's alopecia was getting worse. One night, Victoria came to Donna's room, scared and crying, holding a huge handful of hair and saying she wanted to shave her head. Victoria said she was ready and wanted to donate her hair because there were so many people who were suffering and needed it. Donna told Victoria that it was okay to be sad, and they went to the doctor the next morning. Although the doctor recommended trying a new medicine and using a topper in the meantime, Victoria was not interested. She got a buzz cut and couldn't stop smiling as she sat in the chair. Victoria told the hairdresser that "the sound of the cut was satisfying" and that she felt like she was "cutting her stress away." Since then, Victoria has been wearing bandanas to school, and teachers have been reaching out to Donna to say how brave Victoria is and how she has left an impression on them. The day that Donna thought would be the worst for Victoria turned out to be the best because Victoria took control and now feels empowered. Donna is so proud of Victoria's courage and compassion, even during a traumatic experience.

FORECASTING IS KEY

Until we all were thrust into the shocking experience of a global pandemic, I'd never been able to describe what it feels like to have people overtly steer themselves away from you . . . just for being yourself. Yet the fear of COVID-19 produced some relatable scenes of neighbors playing games of chicken with each other when they approached from opposite directions on the sidewalk. Who would yield first for fear of the other? It reminded me of what I experienced all the time—upon seeing me or my children, mothers or fathers would tug at their own kids to avoid an embarrassing outburst. As a result of the pandemic, it finally seemed like everybody would experience what it felt like to be treated as a pariah by someone else.

I am always grateful for parents of kids who are not different and still resist the impulse to whisk their kids away. The effort pays off in spades for all involved. Once while speaking on a webinar panel, I was asked a question from a military mom.

"Hi, Meg. My daughter often meets people who've been injured during combat. Completely unflustered and forever uber-curious, she constantly asks them about their physical differences. I can feel it in my bones even before it happens, that moment when their obvious disfigurement catches her eye. I hold my breath, secretly praying that just for once she will choose to stay silent. However, my prayers are never answered. 'Excuse me . . .' she always says to each stranger as I cringe inside. I'm wondering if I should've given her a heads-up about the people whose bodies are missing limbs, eyes, even ears, and explain it all to her in advance. Maybe then she wouldn't feel the need to approach them?"

In response, I reassured her, "You're doing the perfect thing for your daughter."

From my vantage point, her daughter was approaching the injured veterans with natural curiosity. This was far preferable to warning her in advance, inflaming her imagination and instilling unnecessary fear. My mind drifted to an experience at a relative's birthday party. With the best of intentions, he had cautioned his five-year-old son to not do anything to make me feel uncomfortable since I was born with hardly any fingers or toes. When I arrived, the boy screamed out in fear at the sight of me. The memory reminds me it's impossible to program young children to fall in line with a parent's desired reaction. I've always preferred people of any age to approach me and my children with an inquisitive mind, even if it meant creating an uncomfortable encounter.

But if that's my advice for people encountering those who are different, it means that my kids need to develop the strength to endure this type of attention and the questions that come with it. Again, that work needs to be done at home. But what is the best approach? I am convinced that one of the most important tools is to arm your child with knowledge of what is to come. It's like giving Wonder Woman her gold cuffs or Captain America his shield. Nobody wants to be blindsided or unprepared for a tough moment. One day after a particularly annoying encounter when a girl wouldn't stop staring at Charlie while we were in line at a store, I decided to provide him additional insight later that evening.

"Okay, Char, when I was little, I realized the kids who noticed my difference were doing the same type of thing."

I proceeded to forecast what he could expect, turning all the anticipated reactions of other children into distinct categories he could understand:

○ The Starers/Whisperers/Pointers: These kids will be very surprised to see your difference. They are not ready, nor do they desire to engage with you at that moment. They may even grab a few friends to show them your difference. Whatever you do, offer a brief smile back as they stare. Or at least make sure to not appear bothered. No. Matter. What. You can even move away if possible, but show them that you don't care what they think. Eventually, they'll get bored.

- **The Curious Georges:** These kids will want to know why you look different and come up and ask you. This is a great thing! It's your chance to ask them questions about themselves, too. Then try telling them you like how they drew a picture or played soccer in recess or . . . you get the drift. The conversation will eventually flow away from your difference to something more interesting for you both.

- **The Bullies:** Be prepared. Some kids will be intentionally mean. They are not feeling good inside and want to make someone else hurt too. Expect them. Know that you cannot force them to be nice to you. They are a waste of your time. Feel sorry for them, since something else is making them unhappy inside that's making them want to torment you.

- **The Scaredy Cats:** They are afraid of your difference. They might even wonder if it is contagious and ask you about it directly, or they may stay away and talk to a parent later. They might even blurt out something that feels mean, but it is not intentional. Don't worry about the Scaredy Cats. The only thing you can do is show them you are living your life and participating with the rest of the class like everyone else. They will eventually forget about being afraid of your difference and may even end up being your friend. It just might take more time.

- **The Heroes:** Some kids will notice your difference but then move on. They are content with themselves and probably will go home and ask their mom or dad why you were born different. That's perfectly fine. These kids will be a gift to you—cherish them when they show up.

By explaining these types of behaviors ahead of time, it was as if I was letting our son in on our own little secret. In fact, when a Curious George or Scaredy Cat would react, sometimes we would just wink and knowingly smile at each other. By helping Charlie anticipate another person's behavior before it happened, I provided him the tools to be better prepared for the next inevitable encounter.

IN ANOTHER'S SHOES

My parents intuitively recognized the importance of helping me put myself in another's shoes to better understand their reactions. For example, when I was five, my family moved to Afghanistan. There, my father did research on the domestic judicial system while my mom taught at the American Cultural Center. After about a week of trying to get acclimated to our new home, where I'd hear the sounds of Dari (the local language) coming through the thin apartment walls and peer over our terrace to witness periodic rioting in the streets, there was a knock on the door. My mother opened it to find an attractive Afghan in her mid-twenties. Her name was Gul Begum and she was there to help take care of my brothers and me. Gul's husband had arranged for her to live and work with us even though they had their own small child. She moved to the spare bedroom in the back of our home, while Gul's mother took care of Gul's child.

On the first day that she arrived to pick us up after school, I couldn't help but stare into Gul's almost pitch-black almond-shaped eyes. But every time I looked at her, she would avoid eye contact. Then, the next morning when I tried to grab onto Gul's hand on our way to school, she avoided touching me and instead took her scarf and tied one end around Teddy's stroller. I held the scarf, not her.

One evening the following week, my brother Peter mistakenly opened the bathroom door when Gul was changing. She laughed, and in her strong accent, reminded him to always knock. A few days later when I raced down the hallway and thrust open the bathroom door to pee, I inadvertently walked in on Gul taking a bath. Her body was totally submerged, but her face was visible, and for the first time our eyes locked for a moment. Then she began to scream. I assumed she had seen a cockroach, so I began to look around, hoping to capture it for her. Her outburst continued until my mother arrived and ushered me out.

Many years later, I learned that Gul was terrified of me, believing that if our eyes met or if she touched my deformities, it would bring evil to her and her family. My family even learned at the end of our stay that Gul Begum wasn't her real name. To share it might bring a curse to her own family. In desperate need of money, she reluctantly convinced herself that as long as she didn't look at me or touch me, she could escape any curse I embodied. Having no other good options, my parents kept her around, hoping she would move past her fear once she got to know me.

And so in addition to experiencing the challenges of living with three very young children in a tumultuous and unstable country, my parents also had to help me figure out how to handle the irrational reactions of others. The evening after the bath incident, as I lay in bed, my mom entered my room and began to stroke my hair.

"Meggie, let's pretend something."

Tired but curious, I waited.

"I want you to pretend that you are Gul Begum, and there, for the first time standing before you, is you. What do you see? How old are you? How tall are you?" And then she added, "How many fingers and toes do you have?"

I hesitated, but then began to describe myself.

"I am five. I am not as tall as Peter but taller than Teddy. I have brown eyes, brown hair, and one finger on each hand . . ."

"Aha!" she interrupted. "Have you ever seen anyone with one finger on each hand, short arms, and one toe on each foot like you?"

I held my breath. I hadn't. Instantly, I understood. By putting myself into Gul's shoes, I began to understand what it might feel like meeting me. It was my turn to interject.

"But, Mommy, you've told me that there is nothing wrong with me."

Pulling the covers up to my neck, she kissed my forehead.

"And that is what we already know and for everyone else to find out."

THE PITY PARTIES

In order for our kids to manage the emotional toll of being different, it's essential that we give them the space to let it out, reset, and recharge. Being them is not always easy; they need to know that we not only get that but are here to help them to recover and move forward.

At age ten, our son Ethan was featured in a magazine with an accompanying photo. In it, he sat in his room with each of his one-fingered hands held up high as if to say, "I got this." The article by Lauren Tarshis, "The Awesome Powers of Ethan Z," described how despite being born with two fingers, Ethan played basketball and video games, rode a bike, and most important, was described to kids as being "just like you." The piece was enthusiastically received by teachers, students, and families across the United States and did a fantastic job of normalizing being different in a relatable way. But while other children are fascinated with the fact that a one-fingered boy can play sports, that same kid is trying to cope with how the world is reacting to him. The toll of stares, finger-pointing, and harsh reactions can become greatly taxing. Periodically your child may feel like enough is enough. Some days are better than others, but on occasion they might come home particularly distraught about their lot in life.

My dad called them "pity parties"—those occasions when I'd become so emotionally frustrated that I'd sob every so often from deep feelings of self-doubt and anxiety in the privacy of my own home. While even an innocent interaction with a stranger could spark a pity party, one could also be triggered by nothing more than simply being tired. In other words, be prepared for your child to have a pity party at any moment.

Whenever my father would hear me bawling, he would come to my room and often gently place his hand on my back, letting me continue to cry . . . but only for a short while. He instinctively knew that while I needed time to air my frustrations, letting me wallow in them wouldn't help me in the long run. After a few minutes of watching me bury my face in my pillow, he'd say something like, "C'mon, Meg. You've had your cry. Now it's time to move on. You are in charge of your own happiness."

He'd then bring me with him to do something to distract me and help me move on. And on the occasions when my mom would come to comfort me, she'd often put her arm around me, holding me close. She'd sometimes use the moment to express something impactful, like, "You know, Meg, life isn't fair for any of us. You just get a chance to deal with it earlier, so you can move on much sooner than most."

SETTING THE TONE

As a parent of a child who is different, I've underscored the importance of taking the lead to shape other people's understanding and perspective of their difference. It's just as important for your child to emulate this approach. If, on the one hand, they present themselves as embarrassed about their lot in life, other kids will feed off their insecurities. On the other hand, if they lead with confidence or even humor, they will find that other kids will become comfortable much sooner.

I'm reminded of Sydney Veloso's older brother Henry, who, upon learning of his own autism diagnosis while in elementary school, wrote an essay for a program I was running. Rather than feeling shame, Henry came out swinging with positivity and humor as he educated his classmates:

Asperger's syndrome! What on earth is Asperger? It sounds like a vegetable! It's caused by a problem in the brain. It makes people think and act differently from others. In 1944, a German doctor named Hans Asperger discovered that some children behaved differently from the majority. He named it after himself (credit hog!). People with Asperger's have problems relating to others. They find it hard to understand what other people are thinking or feeling. And it's hard for them to say what they are thinking or feeling. When they explain things to you, they may leave important bits out. Often, they find something that really interests them, and they will become little Einsteins in that area and will tell you about that subject over and over and over again. In my case it's space. Outer space.

Unfortunately, Asperger's has its dark sides. I have had my fair share of punishments. Once I had to go cold turkey with electronics because I was addicted. A few weeks later, I was banned. In a nutshell, I asked my dad if I could use his iPhone at the regional spelling bee. He relented, and I nearly left my awesome jacket because I was distracted.

Get my drift? Asperger's sometimes distracts me from what I need to do.

It also helps me in school. As you may recall, my Asperger's interest is outer space. I also excel in math and science and similar subjects. My reading level and vocabulary are beyond average, giving me an edge in grammar. Some call me "Conan the Grammarian"! Topic adaptation is one of my many skills, too. Give me a few minutes, and I can figure out anyone's favorite topic! In short, Asperger's enables me and disables me in many ways. For all of you with Asperger's out there, it's not a disease. It's a gift.

Pam Kelly, whose daughter Nicole was born with one arm due to amniotic band syndrome, found another way to help Nikki take control of the conversation about her being different with her peers. Pam was inspired to have her daughter use her condition as a platform to educate other children, rather than avoiding the subject entirely. When Nikki was in kindergarten, she received a prosthetic arm. Pam knew the kids would whisper about it. Rather than waiting for the reactions to flood in, Pam helped Nikki speak about why having a prosthetic was very useful to her. Pam also baked "hand" sugar cookies for Nikki to bring to school. The next day, Nikki was able to speak about the new device to her classmates while they enjoyed their cookies. Afterward, Nikki overheard other kids describing her difference as "cool." Mission accomplished. Nikki now goes by Nicole. She became Miss Iowa and competed in the 2013 Miss America Pageant on behalf of her home state. Now Nicole is a national disability rights advocate, encouraging people of all ages to be proud, fearless, and accepting of themselves and others.

When Ethan was very young, I often overheard him responding with a laugh to inquisitive children, "Oh, I lost 'em in the war . . ." Teaching your kids that they can take the reins with how they view themselves helps to set the tone for other kids. In a nutshell, they are showing other kids that they are just fine with being different, paving the way for others to follow their lead.

THINK OUTSIDE THE BOX

Be creative as you think of ways to strengthen your child's sense of dignity. When your child is very young, your tactics will just seem like fun. But as they grow, coming up with strategies with your child to help them face life's indignities will make them feel that you get it. Sometimes you get to plan in advance, and other times you'll have to wing it.

At about the age of four, I became increasingly bothered that other kids wouldn't stop paying attention to my hands.

"Mommy, I can't make them stop looking at me and asking questions."

My mother took a deep breath and looked as though she were lost in thought. "You must not be my little girl because my little girl has the most beautiful big brown eyes."

I flashed a wide grin. "I have big brown eyes, Mommy!"

"Well, *my* little girl has gorgeous, long, dark brown hair!"

I pointed to my hair with both fingers. "Look, Mommy, I have long, pretty, brown hair!"

She took a breath. "Well, *my* little girl is very smart and always smiles a lot!"

"I smile a lot, Mommy!"

Finally, after a long pause, she said, "But how can you be my little girl? My little girl has two fingers, one on each hand."

"Me! Me! Me! I have one finger on my hands!" I waved them high in the air, almost frantically, in her face.

"Oh! Then you *must* be my darling daughter, Meggie!"

We embraced. I would ask my mother to play that game with me again and again.

Decades later, as soon as Ethan could understand, I began to play "My Little Boy" with him, delighted as he excitedly waved his own two tiny fingers in the air with pride. I've found that the same game my own mother played with me became one of the building blocks necessary to teach our children self-love. In fact, the renowned American psychologist Paul Ekman, my husband John's cousin who served as a guide when I was developing our nonprofit's national SEL (social and emotional learning) programming in schools, explained to me that the best way to teach children is to approach them with a game that they enjoy and that is also instructive. My mother was onto something.

When Ethan decided he wanted to play YMCA soccer in our hometown, the idea sounded great to me, but was also mixed with a strong element of "Oh, crap. Here we go . . ." At the end of every game, the opposing teams would line up and walk past each other exchanging high-fives. After Ethan's first game, one player after another raised or lowered their hand to avoid touching Ethan's small, one-fingered hands. Although the "My Little Boy" game had been an important stepping-stone, I knew it would be insufficient in these circumstances, and I'd have to get more creative.

When we returned home that night, I followed Ethan to his room. I saw the center of his pillow was moist and stained from his tears.

"I can't stop them from moving away from me, Mommy. They don't want to touch my hands. I hate my hands!" At that, he sobbed even harder.

"Here's the deal, E. Have you ever considered that everyone in the soccer line is treating one another with respect by slapping each other's hands, even though they didn't earn or deserve it? Ethan, you automatically deserve to be respected. But you don't necessarily get it as easily as most. That's just the way it is for us."

I continued, "Ethan, any kid who pulls away from you is just surprised or acting out of fear about something they've never seen. Have you ever noticed that anyone who gets to know you loves to be with you? They don't focus on your hands, and they just treat you like everyone else. Those are the kids who matter."

He nodded.

"Next time, let's make our own game out of this. Let's count how many kids from the opposing team high-five you and how many don't."

I paused. "I guess there will be seven kids who avoid your hands."

Ethan smiled and replied, "I think there will be six."

The next weekend, Ethan scored his first goal. To make the moment even sweeter, Ethan's coach gave him an "atta boy," accompanied by a high-five, while his teammates ran up to him and cheered. At the end of the game, Ethan's team had won by two goals. As the kids lined up for high-fives, Ethan looked over at me and mouthed, "Six," as I mouthed back, "Seven." According to Ethan's count, we were both mistaken. Only five kids avoided his hands. Ethan wasn't even bothered by the kids who wouldn't touch him.

Pam Kelly shares another successful strategy she used to support her daughter. Whenever the family was in a public place and people would whisper and stare at Nikki, the family had an inside joke. Pam would start talking loudly about the great "shark attack" as the family laughed together. This game alleviated Nikki's feelings of awkwardness and alienation and helped her to put things in perspective—she could even laugh and have fun.

My friend Debbie Kass's daughter, Chloe, at age five, became paralyzed and unable to breathe on her own due to a virus. One day, when they were visiting a rehabilitation center, a doctor called Chloe "floppy" to her face. Understandably, the description made Chloe cry instantly. But rather than having Chloe wallow in sadness, Debbie immediately sprang into action. On the car ride home, they made up a song that they sang together repeatedly: "I'm not floppy, I am strong, and I'm not going down, down, down to the ground . . ."

Although the doctor's insensitivity upset Chloe, it also motivated the family to find a creative way to help Chloe quickly move past the experience, teaching her the important lesson to not get stuck in sadness or self-pity, and empowering Chloe with essential tools to move on.

LESSONS IN MEDIA AND ENTERTAINMENT

Unfortunately, for decades, people who are different have been portrayed in films, TV shows, and books as everything from misfits to monsters. And though there is definitely a conscious effort in the television and film industry to update their attitudes about traditional prejudices, unintentional mistakes are still made. Just recently, my kids and I were horrified when a mainstream movie likened having a limb difference and being bald with being evil. After swift public backlash, the studio and film's director issued a statement: "We are deeply saddened to learn that our depiction of the fictional characters . . . could upset people with disabilities, and regret any offense caused. . . . It was never the intention for viewers to feel that the fantastical, non-human creatures were meant to represent them. This film is about the power of kindness and friendship. It is our hope that families and children can enjoy the film and embrace this empowering, love-filled theme."

Given the film's purported goal, I found it particularly ironic that it caused anxiety and embarrassment among our kids who are different and reinforced negative stereotypes about them. The studio's hopes fell flat. As I wrote in a piece in *The Mighty*, "As a parent of children who are physically different, I felt the demonic imagery from the film was at best deeply insensitive and at worst destructive to impressionable kids learning to accept their bodies. It sends just the wrong cues, making children who are different objects of fear just as they are desperate to fit into their social world."

So if these hiccups are inevitable, and there is no question that our children will encounter harmful stereotypes in media and entertainment, what can be done?

When my kids were very young, I exposed them to age-appropriate films that provided them encouragement and insight. In *Rudolph the Red-Nosed Reindeer* (1964), not only does Rudolph learn that his glowing red nose would actually turn out to be his greatest asset, the relationship between Rudolph and his elf friend, Hermey, is just as meaningful. Although outwardly Hermey is cute as a button, his "difference," as he explains to Rudolph, is his strong desire to become a dentist, rather than make toys. Hermey feels tremendous pressure to hide his true self and fears others' reactions to him. Initially, both Rudolph and Hermey are bullied into conformity. The two relate to each other because of, not despite, their differences. Rudolph provides the depth of understanding that someone seemingly "perfect" could also consider themselves different and feel inferior. There is so much power in helping your child understand that while they might look blatantly different, they also have peers who feel different, too. In *Finding Nemo* (2003), Nemo the clownfish learns to describe his deformed, small fin as "lucky" to help with his confidence. But I think my heart melted the most when an octopus friend named Pearl inclusively highlights her own shorter tentacle, which prompts Sheldon the seahorse to chime in, "I'm H_2O-intolerant!" These types of films beautifully introduce messages of inclusion, re-silience, and unity.

But as my children grew older, directing them to PG-rated films became inadequate, since they would confront errors in judgment in the media whether I was around or not. The key was engagement, so I employed my own "Involve Me and I'll Learn" methodology. In other words, while I couldn't prepare them for every troubling or offensive thing they read or saw, I'd be ready to talk through things with them as the need arose. I didn't want to raise angry, resentful kids, though, so when some new show or film included an offensive element, I made sure to remain calm with my own reaction and explain that someone who didn't have a difference or parent a child with a difference simply didn't understand our perspective—it didn't matter whether they were a famous director or ran a large movie studio. I explained that we ought to give them the benefit of the doubt.

To invite a thoughtful response to portrayals of difference in pop culture and the media, you can ask your child questions such as:

- Was there anything about the film/show that made you feel good inside?

- Describe a moment when you felt uneasy or sad.

- What would you have done differently if you were the director or writer?

- Would you have changed the ending?

- What would you want to say to the director?

If my kids and I felt particularly upset about a story line or the way a character was portrayed, we'd write a letter together, sharing what we enjoyed about the movie as well as expressing our concerns. When they were old enough, I'd even encourage them to write down their feelings independently. Even if we didn't feel compelled to actually send the letter, they learned how to articulate why they deserved the same level of respect as everyone else.

Helping a child who is different have a voice is a step toward their unconditional self-acceptance. And when the next insensitive thing rolls along, they are either ready to express themselves or have the strength to not be fazed.

"INSPIRING" DOESN'T HAVE TO MEAN "DISEMPOWERING"

To be honest, even into adulthood, I deeply resented when anyone described me as "inspiring." I've been told by a stranger in line behind me at the grocery store that I am an inspiration for grabbing my wallet out of my purse to pay. And I know I am not alone. I've read that many people in the disability community share that same feeling. Once, a student who uses a wheelchair was told by a college professor that she was his "hero" for showing up to class on time. It is extremely frustrating to hear someone describe you as courageous or inspirational when you're simply living your life in the way that is most familiar and comfortable to you. As a child, I never discussed this feeling with my parents, but I silently brooded in frustration any time someone would foist the term "inspiring" on me. And there's irony in the whole dynamic. Those same people are actually saying it to make those they encounter with a visible difference or disability feel great. But when anyone is impressed by something you don't think twice about, it feels belittling. It's our life's paradox.

After I became a mother of children who share my condition, I knew they'd find themselves in the same boat. Should I teach them to ignore the praise? Should they correct the person, explaining that whatever they were doing wasn't truly a big deal? In order to help our boys through this inevitable scenario, I needed to figure out the best approach—and it came neither intuitively nor easily for me. An experience with Ethan helped me to figure it out.

The summer after fourth grade, Ethan attended a basketball camp. As much as he loved to play the sport, this was the first time we'd sent him to any type of sports-only camp. In my heart, I knew that spending five hours a day not only playing ball but learning technique would push our eldest son, both physically and socially. At the end of the first day, I called home from work.

"How was it, hon?"

"Mom, it's okay, but I don't think I love it."

"How come?"

"I don't know, just because."

I didn't press. I could only imagine the volume of stares and unwelcome attention he endured on his first day, in his first hour, his first minutes. By the second day, when I called again, Ethan's voice had brightened, and he seemed to be enjoying his time much more. I decided not to ask for details unless he volunteered.

On the last day, my husband and I sat in the bleachers with all the other parents for an all-camp ceremony where the coaches handed out different awards for varying talent. I hadn't even known there was a basketball technique called "the Spider," but there was an award for it. Just the day before, Ethan boasted that he had figured out how he could do the maneuver, even with his small palm and one finger.

The head coach began to tell a story of a girl named Cindy Lowe. Apparently, he had been coaching her fourth-grade team years ago and was extremely upset over a narrow loss.

"Excuse me, Coach," Cindy said to him. "I thought it wasn't about whether we win or lose, but how we play the game?"

Apparently, the comment impacted the coach and helped him put the game in perspective. Cindy went on to become a great basketball player in high school, but at the age of twenty-two, she became ill and tragically died from cancer.

He continued. "And so, in honor of Cindy, we have a Most Inspirational Player Award." My heart sank. "Here it comes," I thought.

"And the Most Inspirational Player Award goes to . . . Ethan Zucker!"

Loud applause. And there, among the hundreds of people gathered, our ten-year-old son walked up from his bleacher seat to receive his plaque and smile for the camera. Admittedly, my own inner child felt annoyed.

"Of course the two-fingered kid has to win this," I thought to myself.

I knew they meant well but wondered why this award couldn't be given to a typical child. Didn't Ethan instead deserve the "Most Improved Player Award"? When Ethan approached me afterward, I gave him a hug but wondered if he felt the way I did. Later that evening I shared my thoughts with John.

"If Ethan didn't have one finger on each hand, I'm positive he wouldn't have won this. On the court he's just like everyone else."

Like any supportive, amazing husband, John provided me with perspective.

"Meg, you know handling a basketball is not easy for a kid with only one finger. It's very hard to control the ball and dribble with one hand like he does. And he's a more consistent shooter than I ever was. Whether you like it or not, the fact that Ethan plays the sport, loves it, and is even relatively good at it, is inspirational. He is *not* just like everyone else. You need to swallow that pill and move past it."

I couldn't sleep for a long time that night. John's words rang in my ears. I needed to check my pride at the door and allow others to recognize our differences and accept them favorably. Although we don't feel particularly special for accomplishing the things we can physically achieve, there is clearly an upside. Ethan was recognized and felt accomplished for something that many would not even expect him to try. And, more important, his winning the award might push some kids harder, beyond their own assumed limitations. The short kid might just try to jump all the higher. The slower kid might just try to run faster. The star athlete might even be more open to passing the ball to a kid who didn't seem to be as strong a player. Building my child's self-confidence included accepting the fact that he had a role to play in motivating others. Ethan attended the same basketball camp for the next four years, and every summer he would continue to be awarded the same recognition, creating a running joke in our family.

Since then, using real examples we have experienced, I make sure to explain to my children in the privacy of our own home that they have the power to motivate others. And most important, using that lens can even be self-fulfilling. Let's face it, other people will continue to describe them as inspiring, whether we resent it or not. Since they can inspire others just by being themselves, the lesson for our kids who are different is that they have a noble role to play, and their difference is a gift that keeps on giving. Because it motivates others, being called an inspiration is a price we can be willing to pay.

DIGNITY TOOLS

You are your child's strongest and most important advocate. While it's important to help them develop go-to language about what makes them unique, teaching them tricks to deflect is just as important.

I like to equip my kids with visual tools to remind them that they have control over their own happiness. One example involves asking your child to draw a ladder (or helping them draw one, depending on their age). I call it a "Dignity Ladder" and share with them the following:

"Sometimes when we wake up, we won't feel as happy about being different as on other days. That is when we are at the bottom of the Dignity Ladder. It's up to us to get back to the top of the ladder."

I then ask them to draw a picture of themselves at the very top. If they are not artistically inclined, it also works to glue a photo of them to the top of the ladder. In either case, we next draw a crown on their head.

"When we are at the top of our ladder, it means we don't care what other kids or people think about us. It is the best, most beautiful place to be. But only *we* can climb to the top of the Dignity Ladder. Some days we will start at the top, but other days it will be harder. Every day our goal is to get there."

Another visual I used with Ethan is what I call the "Car Game."

"E, imagine you are riding with me and Dad in a convertible. It's a picture-perfect, sunny warm day. We're about to do something you love, like going to the beach. But all of a sudden, there is a downpour. And because you're in the convertible, you get soaked in the rain."

Having grabbed his attention, I continued. "Now, change the image. You're in a regular car with a roof, and the same storm bursts through the sky. Do you get wet?"

Ethan grinned. "Nope."

Here was my chance.

"Exactly. Just think of the storm as people saying things to you that make you feel uncomfortable or even hurt your feelings. You can't stop these outbursts from coming, just like you can't stop the rain. When they come your way, however, just picture yourself in the second type of car, with the roof covering you."

This concept resembled the swing analogy I had given to Charlie when he was around the same age, but that was the point. The lessons and visuals would be reinforced in different ways, with the same goal in mind: Helping children who are different focus on the things they could control so they didn't feel helpless, and in the process, building their self-worth. Embracing their dignity was not only crucial, it needed to become second nature.

Whether you use my dignity tool examples or make up your own, which I also encourage, your kids will feel better equipped to manage their daily lives. My parents never actually told me that they were using their own arsenal of tools to help me overcome the inevitable judgment of others. They unconditionally supported me in ways that made sense for my emotional growth. In turn, I have tried to lead all three of my children down the same dignified path to help them blossom, always channeling one of my favorite quotes from President Abraham Lincoln: "No man is good enough to govern another man without that other's consent."

CHAPTER 3

Let Go and Let Live

When I was around one, my mother brought me to my annual checkup. Most babies my age were already holding their own bottles and beginning to walk, but unsurprisingly I was physically delayed. During the examination, when the doctor asked my mom a question, she lifted her hand away from me for a split second. In that instant, I rolled off the table headfirst. But instead of my skull being shattered on the tile floor, I fell upside down into a small, skinny wastebasket. Miraculously, it was full of soft packaging materials. Crying, upside down with my feet kicking up in the air, remarkably I was unharmed! My mother rushed to grab me while the doctor sat down, his face unnaturally pale. After examining me, he placed his hand gently on my mother's shoulder.

"My goodness! That Meggie is one lucky baby. Looks like we don't need to fear for her future. Just stand back and watch her conquer."

The doctor's words would serve as a guidepost and translated to our family's motto: Let go and let live. In following this directive, my parents purposefully held back, allowing me to explore what was possible. This approach is not necessarily intuitive for most, however. Once when I was young, a relative said something alarming to me: "Meg, thank goodness *your* parents raised you. I would have never let you out of my sight."

I instantly visualized myself stuck in my house, unable to do anything or go anywhere unless accompanied by my mom or dad. Wanting to support your child is understandable and warranted, but excessively steering their life and overprotecting them is more harmful than helpful. Yet it would be unfair for me to judge. As a parent of kids who are different, I soon learned how hard it was to resist leaping to the rescue. We as parents want to thwart potential failure and ensure success for our kids, or so we tell ourselves. I wonder if sometimes my need for them to avoid missteps is more about me and my fear of failure than theirs. Fear often led me to thoughts such as:

- What might happen if I don't do a, b, or c?

- They won't be able to accomplish x, y, or z without me.

- I'll just help them this one time.

- They couldn't possibly do that on their own.

- I don't want them to appear helpless.

- I have to show them first.

- They need me.

Being an overprotective parent doesn't necessarily translate as unconditional love. Helicopter-style parenting can easily lead to harm. If we show our children that they need us to figure things out, then the message we're sending is that they shouldn't try new things on their own. We're giving them the cue that we don't trust them to explore and take healthy risks.

It's all too easy for parents of young children to yield to the temptation to overprotect because little ones will usually let you overstep. As far as they know, you're just doing your job as their parent. The potential consequences for children with perceived or actual physical challenges can be more severe than for the general population. For those learning to live or newly adapt to life with a difference, the unwarranted help creates dependency and stifles potential. The risk of your approach backfiring is great.

One day when I was eight years old, I was feeling particularly mortified after having to ask my dad to tie my shoes outside of the dressing room in front of my friends at our local swimming club. Until that point, I hadn't been encouraged to learn to tie them, like my ten-fingered sibling, Peter. While my parents generally understood the importance of refraining from intervention, at times they too simply couldn't fathom how I'd be able to maneuver a task with only one finger on each hand. After the shoelace incident, I wailed when I got home, frustrated at my own lack of independence and feeling humiliated. That afternoon, rather than explaining to me why they needed to continue to help me with my laces, my parents left me alone for hours in my room so I could figure it out on my own. And to my and everyone's delight, I did.

"Let go and let live" means giving your child the freedom to try the unimaginable, even if it means they might fail. Maybe they will and maybe they won't. It's okay either way. And there is an additional upside. When I was given the freedom to try something I couldn't be taught, my creative juices were triggered—something that would benefit me later in life as a person who could always approach challenges with ingenuity. Like a boxing coach, my parents prepared me to step out into life's ring, while still being there when I needed them after every round. Had they raised me any other way, I am convinced I would likely have become a more reserved, apprehensive, physically limited adult, rather than the self-assured person I am now. Every child deserves the same support to live to their full potential.

RELINQUISHING CONTROL

For a parent of a child who is different, abdicating control can feel like the hardest, riskiest thing ever. But if irrational fear is the only reason you are holding your child back, increasing their level of independence has value beyond comparison. And let's face it, when they're older and realize you stifled or delayed their potential, they can easily feel resentful.

I've thought a lot about the word "conquer"—it can apply to both small- and large-scale accomplishments. It could mean successfully overcoming something as mundane as a math problem, or achieving something substantial—like climbing a mountain. As the parent of a child who is different, you want to do everything humanly possible to help them overcome their actual or perceived limitations. You're anxious to fix things so that they get a chance to begin life's race at the same starting line as others. But for children who were born different, they have never known anything else. So their own starting line is exactly what is familiar to them—they just need the freedom to try. And when they succeed? It feels extraordinary to conquer something that everyone presumed was practically impossible, like climbing Mount Everest. By stepping back, you are accepting that sometimes your best role is to be a cheerleader on the sidelines, rooting for them. And being open to the possibility that you don't always know what's best or truly possible for them to achieve should make it easier for you to take a deep breath and hold back, too.

One of my earliest memories was driving nearly three hours with my parents to the University of Illinois College of Medicine's Rehabilitation Clinic in Chicago. The goal of the clinic was to help people with amputations or limb deficiencies achieve the best quality of life. It was no wonder my mom and dad brought me there, believing a prosthetic would make my life much easier. How would I be able to use only one finger to write with a pencil or cut with scissors? With no personal experience to draw upon, they were convinced that without more fingers or an opposable thumb for grasping, I'd likely live a significantly limited life. The journey to the clinic gave them hope.

Sitting in the waiting room between my parents and holding each of their hands, I looked around nervously. Although I saw other kids who had blatant physical differences too, as far as I could tell, nobody else had my specific difference. Some were missing entire limbs, or instead of a full arm had only a finger or two hanging from a shoulder or elbow. Strange as it may sound, having never met anyone with an extreme physical difference, I was startled by the sight of *them*. (Years later I'd learn that those birth defects likely resulted from their mothers taking thalidomide during pregnancy to treat severe morning sickness. The drug was pulled from the market only after its disastrous side effects had afflicted thousands.) Finally, the nurse beckoned me over to see the doctor. Hearing my name called aloud caused an additional jolt of anxiety that enveloped me. The doctor greeted the three of us without looking at my face, staring instead at my body. I felt like an object. He then spoke to me directly.

"You're extremely lucky to be born now. People in the past had to wear prosthetics made from wood taken from their furniture."

Apparently, that was where the term "peg leg" came from—but I was too young to grasp what he was saying, and anyway, in no mood for a history lesson. The doctor proceeded to hold up a prosthetic made from an uncomfortable combination of rubber, plastic, and metal. Even worse, it looked incredibly fake. To me, the device, and not me, looked abnormal. Appearance aside, once the doctor began to try to attach it, I detested how it felt. He tried several times to fit the first one onto my right hand, but I resisted and thwarted his attempts. All I could think of was that wearing the prosthetic would hamper my ability to do anything. I instantly hated it, and by transference, him. With my anger rising, I began to thrash my arm so hard that the prosthetic was hurled across his office and banged into the wall before crashing to the ground. Picking it up, he then explained to my parents that this type of behavior was normal and attempted to convince me to try it on again. But I was defiant and refused. He then turned to my parents for backup.

To my utter relief, my dad instead looked at my mom and then at me and said, "Let's go home."

Although I was extremely young, I worried that I had disappointed my parents. And yet, I was also overjoyed by their decision to leave the rehab clinic without fitted prosthetics. While prosthetics can be an important asset depending on a person's needs, my parents' willingness to follow my instincts meant the world to me. This was one of the earliest examples of how they took a deep breath, gathered their courage, relinquished control, and let me be me.

LET YOUR CHILDREN FAIL

Parents of kids who are not different don't think twice when their child expresses interest in sports, dance, or music. These parents don't have to worry about whether it's physically possible for their child to play an instrument, but they may be anxious to discover the extent of their child's potential talent. The corollary to relinquishing control is being willing to let them fail again and again as they explore what might be possible. When I was growing up, my mom and dad allowed me to explore my every whim, even when they were absolutely certain that what I desired was not physically possible. For example, I'd always loved to swim. My goal was to join the swim team at our summer pool club. But my parents knew that with my shortened forearms and lack of hand width, competing against other kids wasn't realistic. Nonetheless, they refrained from blocking my efforts. Although the coach allowed me to try out for the team, my swim times were too slow to compete. The experience was disappointing, but it wasn't devastating. Later at home that night, I began to brainstorm with my parents about other things I might be able to do. They were consistently my quiet advocates in every context. By letting me explore things they knew were probably or definitely out of reach, my parents were signaling that they trusted me enough to try.

You would think the road map they laid out for me would help me raise my own children. Yet I had quite a hard time consistently emulating their laid-back approach and messed up on multiple occasions. I loathed seeing our sons experience physical failures or embarrassment, especially in front of their peers. For example, when Ethan and Charlie were in elementary school, I shuddered at the possibility that they'd find themselves struggling to open a package of chips in front of their classmates. Yielding to my worst enemy, fear, I thought I would help them avoid any humiliation by pre-opening the bags before putting them in their lunch boxes. I'd pre-open their Poland Spring water bottles, too. In contrast, John was agitated whenever he encountered me trying to make their lives physically easier.

"What the heck, Meg. Let them figure it out on their own."

My efforts backfired, and for a long time our boys assumed

they couldn't open things even though they were actually capable. The reality is that I continued intervening in similar ways for years. I wanted to create the façade of success, even if it wasn't real. The irony of my own failings in this regard is not lost on me.

In fact, years later in high school speech and debate, Ethan mentioned my error in judgment in his award-winning Original Oratory that he delivered at the National Speech and Debate Association tournament. He again mentioned my mistakes in his remarks before hundreds of guests at an event for the nonprofit I founded. As he told it, it took an incident of near dehydration while on a long bike ride for him to finally figure out that he could in fact twist open a water bottle with his one-fingered hands. He's still blaming me for that one. I hope by my 'fessing up now, others won't repeat this type of mistake at their own kids' expense.

And, okay, my parents weren't *always* perfect in this regard, either. For example, my dad zipped up my jacket for me into my late teens, leading me to presume it was something I couldn't do. When I moved away to attend the University of Wisconsin–Madison for college, I walked around campus in snowstorms and minus-ten-degree windchill with my coat open. It took a particularly awful blizzard that began while I was in a lecture hall atop Bascom Hill for me to figure out a way to zip up my own coat before walking back to my dorm. My father, even with the best of intentions, had seriously delayed me.

Letting our children fail means that even if it turns out they are incapable of doing something, they learn to live with it. Or maybe they actually are capable but just need to struggle more than most to figure it out. Most important, they need the opportunity to try.

Letting them fail also means holding yourself back from rushing in for the save. When Ethan and Charlie were much younger, my mom and I brought them to a park, with Savanna coming along in a stroller. While we watched the boys play, my mother recalled a story of when I was a child and fell from the monkey bars. Out of the corner of her eye, she'd observed kids staring and pointing at me. She suppressed the desire to run over to me, however.

"How could you not have come to my rescue?" As a mother, I couldn't fathom it.

Her reply was sincere and uncomplicated.

"Meg, what happens is meant to happen. I couldn't always be there for you, so I needed to let you figure that out. Your father and I believed that always helping you wasn't really helping you."

Sometimes helping your child is not helping them at all. Be conscious of this and always consider it before you rush for the save, especially in front of their friends as they grow older.

My friend Mindy Scheier shared a story about her son, Oliver, who was born with muscular dystrophy and had started progressively losing his physical capabilities. One day when he was in seventh grade, Mindy was dropping Oliver off at a friend's house. Without giving it a second thought, she jumped out of the car and put her arm around him to support him up the steps. It was at that moment that Oliver's friend appeared at the door. Later that evening, Oliver pleaded with her to hold back.

"Mom, I need to figure this out on my own."

Reflecting on the day, Mindy was resolved to let him retain his independence.

"As much as it tears me up inside watching him struggle when I know I can be of help, I remind myself that this is not about me."

EMPOWER YOUR CHILDREN TO FOLLOW THEIR PASSIONS

For me, ballet dancing was both a passion and an aspiration since my mom used to dance en pointe in her youth. I was well aware that the balance necessary for ballet would be nearly impossible on my tiny feet. Also, the delicate slippers fit better hanging on my ears than on those misshapen feet. Yet, my folks picked up on my excitement and never shared any reservations about my determination to dance. Not only did they encourage me, my mom even taught the ballet class I attended when we lived in Pakistan. In doing that, she made sure I'd be afforded every opportunity the other little girls would experience. And when I also expressed an interest in gymnastics, I found myself happily tumbling to my greatest ability. By supporting my every desire, my parents empowered me to actualize a normal, joyful life that tapped into what I cared about. I wish I could say that in this respect I followed their lead.

Some years back, John, the kids, and I went to the apartment of a close friend's grandmother named Beatsie, who was giving away her baby grand piano.

"I'm sure you'll put better use to it than I would these days,"

Beatsie remarked, looking at Savanna, our only ten-fingered child.

Although growing up I had plunked keys here and there to accompany my singing, I jumped to the conclusion that it made sense for only Savanna to take formal piano lessons. On the day of her first lesson, the teacher sat with our daughter and began to teach her about the fundamental concepts of reading music. But as I walked past, I noticed Charlie sitting in the living room, wistfully watching his sister as she began to play. Or was I misreading his expression? At first, I tried to convince myself that perhaps Charlie was just longing for Savanna to finish so they could play in the yard. Deep down, I suspected the truth. He had a natural affinity for music. At Savanna's next lesson the following week, my right eye began to nervously twitch when I noticed him again sitting on the sofa with the same downcast expression, watching her play.

A few weeks later, I heard "Mary Had a Little Lamb" being played beautifully from downstairs.

"Savanna!" I shouted. "Great job! That sounded awesome!"

But then our nanny called out, "Meg, Savanna's taking a bath."

Charlie had learned the song on his own just by listening to his sister play. That night, I phoned the piano teacher, as I should've done from the beginning.

"Hi. I am wondering if you might have interest in giving Charlie lessons, too. Do you think you might be open to being creative . . . ?"

Without missing a beat, she replied, "I thought you'd never ask."

The end-of-year recital was held at a local church. The piano teacher had rented the space and prepared a program for her many students. I noticed several kids in the front two rows who seemed to know one another and were awaiting their turn to play. Meanwhile, Charlie and Savanna sat with us. When it was his turn to perform in front of everyone, Charlie walked to the front and began to play "Happy" by Pharrell Williams. Focused on his playing, Charlie didn't notice a few of the kids in the front row pointing and whispering about his hands. It took every bit of my self-control to not walk up and reprimand them during his performance or at least find their parents to complain. Meanwhile, Charlie was onstage, joyfully playing.

A few months later, Savanna quit, while Charlie would go on to play the piano better than most kids I'd heard. It pains me to think I wasn't paying attention to something that clearly delighted him. The point is that sometimes a child will self-advocate, but it's also important to recognize silent expressions of yearning.

Whether it came to music or sports, I had a lot to learn about giving my kids the opportunity to pursue their passions. One day in second grade, Charlie asked us if he could play on a Little League baseball team. I simply couldn't imagine how he'd be able to wear a glove on his two-fingered hands. So rather than allowing him to explore something he seemed excited about, I effectively forced him to conform to my expectations.

"How about basketball?" I suggested.

By the end of the day, I had signed Charlie up to join the same basketball camp Ethan had been attending for the last two summers. But instead of enjoying it, Charlie came home unfulfilled and frustrated.

The following spring, Charlie again asked if he could try baseball, and again I hesitated. I couldn't imagine how he could play on a team. But then I remembered living in Cairo and desperately wanting to play basketball. I had expressed a desire to play, but instead the coach offered me the position of "manager" of the seventh-grade girls' team. Before our family moved to Cairo, my brother Peter, our neighbor William, and I had spent countless hours on a dilapidated neighborhood basketball court in Illinois playing H-O-R-S-E and P-I-G. I knew I was a great shot, and I suffered that year in Egypt, watching my friends play while I was resigned to sit on the sidelines. I never even mentioned my yearning to play to my parents, which I should have done since they would have had my back. And here was my own son, absolutely determined to follow his own passion. Who was I to get in his way?

And so I relented. The next day, John took Charlie to a local sporting goods store, with a hope and a prayer to buy a glove. They found one made of synthetic material that was more flexible than a traditional leather baseball glove and allowed Charlie to quickly snap it closed despite not having the grip strength of a kid with a regular-sized palm and five fingers. Charlie played that year and continued throughout most of middle school. Fully committed, he begged us for batting practice lessons at the cages and became a devoted player on his teams. He didn't get to play every position he wanted but, as he liked to point out, he "wasn't the worst." Small victories. That first year, Charlie wrote an essay for my website to help convince us of his determination.

If the Glove Fits
by Charlie Zucker

Hi! I'm Charlie and I am seven. My mom is Meg. Here are some things about me you might want to know. Everyone thinks I have good handwriting. They were all surprised because of the way my hands looked. I love art, Legos, foosball, and video games. Up until now, I have only played soccer and basketball. But they are not my favorites. My favorite sports are archery and baseball. I only play archery at camp and sometimes baseball, but I had never worn a glove. I think my parents did not think it would fit me, so I never got to try.

But when I was in Nantucket, they saw I was a really good hitter. I told them that I liked soccer, but what I really want to try is baseball on a team. My parents were not sure, but I told them let's try. So, when I got back from my vacation, they took me to a sports store and my dad tried different baseball gloves on me. Guess what? The glove fit me even though I have only two fingers on my hands! I told them that now I want to get better, before I start to play in the springtime. I am very excited!

I think I taught my parents that I should always try anything. Now I need to find an archery team somewhere near where I live!

Upon reflection, I am pretty mortified at my behavior, compared to the way my own mother and father deliberately tuned in and didn't hesitate to let me pursue *all* of my interests. Both Charlie and Ethan deserved the same unconditional support, despite my fears of the unknown. I had only allowed them to pursue interests that were within the parameters of my own imagination, rather than theirs. Being my children's greatest advocate meant that I needed to champion more than just the things that I thought were conceivable.

Katie Memmel is a mother whose son Tony was born without his left forearm and hand. Tony thrived because Katie and her husband, Todd, had the courage to follow their son's lead in raising him. Katie reminded me that for some, faith can also be a source of strength.

Tony was born in 1985, before ultrasounds were performed routinely. In the delivery room, Todd and I both felt shocked seeing our son for the first time. But our love for him was immediate and strong. I was twenty-four with no parenting experience to draw from. As I held our firstborn in the hospital, my emotions ran rampant and I questioned Tony's entire future. Would he crawl? Would he get married? I just didn't know. One day, our pastor visited. His hopeful message resonated with me as he said, "God often uses what the world views as weakness and turns it into strength." I prayed that would be true for Tony. I never forgot those words.

Meanwhile, Todd approached fatherhood with more of an "it is what it is" philosophy. He believed, and often assured me, that Tony would figure out how to do whatever he wanted to do in his life. Todd and I together, with our differing outlooks, successfully parented our son into a confident, well-adjusted teen.

At thirteen, Tony approached us and announced with resolve, "I want to get a guitar and learn how to play." We stared at him. Tony had many interests, but playing the guitar? With one hand? I simply could not imagine that. But . . . this wasn't about us; it was what Tony wanted. He'd done the research and quoted the cost at about five hundred dollars. Todd and I promised to talk and get back to him the next day.

One thing was certain. Todd and I were both on the same page and wouldn't discourage Tony from his guitar-playing goal. But we also didn't want to spend five hundred dollars on a guitar that might end up sitting in a closet. We decided to test Tony's determination and challenged him to save up for half. It wouldn't be easy for a thirteen-year-old to earn two hundred fifty dollars, but we needed to know he was serious about this conquest.

He was.

Not only did Tony save gift money from his birthday and Christmas, he accepted every babysitting job that came along. Once he came up with his portion, Todd and I had no choice but to ante up our side of the bargain. I'll never forget taking him to the store where his left-handed Fender Stratocaster waited.

A few weeks later, a guitar teacher told us that "he wouldn't know where to start." Tony was unfazed, and even more determined to think outside the box. His biggest challenge was figuring out how he could teach himself to strum the strings. It was time to be creative. Motivated and unwilling to fail, Tony tried various tapes, socks, kitchen gadgets, and even glue. And once he realized a guitar pick fit perfectly in the crease of his elbow (years later, joking he was literally born with a guitar pick holder), Tony was certain he'd be able to play. Next, he surrounded the pick with a strong duct tape and fastened it to the end of his little arm. This allowed him to strum chords and pluck the strings with assurance that the cast couldn't fall off. It's a method Tony still uses to this day.

By that time, with our son's optimism as our guide and any early skepticism in the rearview mirror, we felt excited to help. Todd and I realized we'd had the power to help make or break our son's dreams. Our faith helped us let go of our fears of what others might view as his weakness. We stepped back, trusted, and watched as our child's resolve only grew stronger.

WHEN TO MAKE YOUR MOVE

Sometimes parents *do* need to step in and intervene on their child's behalf. Figuring out whether or when to intervene isn't always obvious, however. The key is to stay in tune with your child's true needs, not what you assume they need. Karen Guilbault, a parent who wrote about her children for the Don't Hide It, Flaunt It organization, shares a story about her daughter, Faith, that drives this point home.

When our daughter Faith was seven months old, she was diagnosed with cerebral palsy. Almost immediately she started physical therapy, occupational therapy, and speech therapy. Faith also had an eye condition called "strabismus" that meant she had to wear glasses with prisms in them, as well as a patch.

Once when Faith was nine years old, she and I went to watch some of her friends who were at a cheer team practice. On the way home, Faith told me she secretly wished she could join but assumed it was impossible because she has CP and uses a walker. I longed to give her the opportunity and phoned a friend who, through a connection, helped make it happen!

I will never forget the joy in Faith's voice when she called my mother to tell her she was able to join her friend Natalie's cheer team for the local junior football league! She was beyond excited to be a part of something right alongside her friends.

The first year was great since they really focused on learning the sideline cheers at practice. She also got to make new friends that she wouldn't have otherwise known. The second year was more focused on the halftime routines. The new coach was a family friend, which made a huge difference because she knew Faith's strengths and weaknesses and wasn't afraid to challenge her a little more. She really went out of her way to include Faith in the halftime dances and stunts. All Faith could talk about for months was how she got to perform a teddy bear stunt and a thigh hold. She loved to go up on her walker seat with one knee and reach up to the sky, holding her pom-pom in one hand and hanging on to her walker with the other.

One time she had the entire crowd going as she turned the wrong way and was cheering toward nobody.

But then in the third year, another new coach joined, and things took a difficult turn for both Faith and me. There was an even greater focus on the halftime routines, with more stunts, and it left Faith with little to do. Most of the time Faith sat on her walker seat just watching all the other girls work on their stunt routine, and I could see the look of disappointment and sadness on her face. Watching these practices usually made my heart hurt, and I would take a deep gulp when I felt my stomach tightening into knots.

It was hitting Faith hard to see all the things the other girls could do that she could not, and she began to feel a little less included and to come down hard on herself. These are the moments that you would never wish on your children, when you want to take away all the pain, hurt, and fear that they might be feeling. Faith and I would just talk it out, and I would continue to encourage her and tell her to look at how much fun she was still having at the games. After all, the halftime routine was just a short part of the game, and Faith continued to cheer on the sidelines the rest of the time.

Looking back on it now, I am glad I spent time at home speaking with Faith so she could confide in me how she felt. I needed her to hear me acknowledge that she needed to work twice as hard as others at certain things. And although the new coach had the best of intentions, I regret not pulling her aside and asking her if there was a little something we could do to better include Faith. It's possible she didn't know how to approach me and simply felt awkward.

PARTNER WITH YOUR POD

Even close family members such as grandparents, aunts, and uncles might presume that your child should be overprotected while in their care. Partner with your pod by sharing your let-go-and-let-live approach and overall disdain of fear-driven parenting. Your child will greatly benefit from everyone being on the same page. Otherwise, inconsistent or conflicting messages may sow confusion, resentment, agitation, and insecurity. A close family member may not have your same fears anyway, and this can actually work in your child's favor!

When my friend Jill and her husband, Nick, discovered their daughter, Parker, had been born with cone dystrophy with supernormal rod response, they were devastated. At the age of four, Parker was already legally blind, with corrected vision at only 20/200. A few months later, Nick was diagnosed with multiple myeloma and given three to five years to live. They made the emotionally fraught decision to treat Nick's illness aggressively, requiring Jill and Nick to move to Arkansas for seven months while leaving Parker (age five) and her brother Carson (age one) with a combination of nannies, grandparents, and Jill's sister, Susan. The phrase "It takes a village" became much more real for them in this season—Jill had to learn to let go and trust her sister implicitly.

Susan and her husband, Carlos, took Parker and Carson on all types of adventures. But Carlos took this to an entirely new level when he taught his two daughters and Parker to ride dirt bikes. In addition to the itty-bitty riding gear, helmets, boots, and matching gloves, he bought them the world's tiniest dirt bikes. Although Susan updated Jill on this escapade, it didn't really register: dirt bike = motorcycle. When Jill came to visit the kids one weekend, she was simultaneously horrified and ecstatic to discover Parker astride her bike.

If she hadn't left the kids, Jill doubts she would ever have let Parker step so far out of her safe haven. Susan and Carlos, however, only saw opportunities and not obstacles for Parker. They treated Parker just like her cousins, alleviating any fears and doubts. Ten years later, Nick thankfully is in remission, and Parker can ride on a treacherous mountain road at high speeds, dodging rocks and tree roots, and across a snowy desert trail where most of us would be blinded by the reflective sunlight. To hear Parker describe it, although her sight is so poor that she has to hold her cell phone within three inches of her nose to read a text, she is unafraid of what she cannot see, and there's no greater thrill for her than trying something new that she loves.

And what about relying on others besides family or close friends to help out? As long as they've been thoroughly vetted and you're certain your child is safe, you'd be wise to let them in on your let-go-and-let-live philosophy, too. Of course, it takes a leap of faith and an additional layer of strength to have anyone else join your child's team. But if you can muster the strength to trust in them, they may become another resource providing your child further opportunities to grow.

For example, a mother named Kimber Felton has a daughter Kate who was born with spastic diplegia, a condition that comes with a mix of physical and mental challenges. When her kids were young, and Kimber was looking for a babysitter, she presumed a mature adult with lots of experience in special education would be best for all involved. But, Kimber admits, "They were chewed up and spit out by Kate."

Once, Kimber arrived home to find a sitter, who was also a special education teacher, crying on the couch because Kate had been mean to her. Meanwhile, Kate's two "mini-spy" siblings defended their sister while questioning the sitter's ability to treat Kate like the rest of the family. According to Kimber, the real problem was that she didn't trust the babysitter enough. Kate didn't need someone who made her feel like she was sitting in a jail cell at home. The sitter watched her every move, not even letting Kate go into the bathroom or her bedroom by herself. Every time she began to enjoy herself, the sitter told her to sit down on the couch. Kate's life was already consumed with people hovering over her in the same way at school. At home, Kate longed for a sitter who would loosen the reins and just let her have fun.

Since the current approach was failing, Kimber decided to pivot by letting go of her stringent requirements and opening up the field of potential babysitters. They found Delaney, a high school junior whom Kimber's youngest daughter called "Delady with the long hair and the braids." Delaney was social and bright and had a quick smile, and nothing fazed her. As they slowly transitioned Delaney into the role, Kimber began to see how nice it was to have an easygoing babysitter. The environment was fun and relaxed. Delaney laughed at the kids' antics, used a lot of reverse psychology, made up cool games, baked brownies, and never took their actions personally. Most important, Delaney treated Kate no differently than the other kids, which was best for all three of Kimber's children.

After about a year of having Delaney babysit, Kimber and her husband felt comfortable enough to go away for a 24-hour trip to New York City. At seven a.m., the phone unexpectedly rang. Kimber's heart was in her mouth, as she imagined the worst. Delaney assured them she had it under control, but there had been a small electrical fire in the basement. Delaney had gotten the kids outside, called 911, and the firemen came and dealt with it. Delaney added that the firemen were "hot" and nice, and then passed the phone to Kate. All Kate could talk about were the gorgeous firemen; she was absolutely fine. Her two siblings were perfectly happy and acted like having firemen come to your house early in the morning was normal. Kimber and her husband stayed and enjoyed the rest of their getaway.

YOU DON'T HAVE ALL THE ANSWERS

Sometimes I think about how the smartest people in the room are the ones who are quietly listening and absorbing everything that is being said around them. Their thoughts and opinions derive from knowledge that has been meticulously collected and curated. When you listen, you become a better decision-maker. I'm reminded that although I'm my children's biggest advocate, that doesn't mean I have all the answers when it comes to their needs, even if I believe I do. With this in mind, ask yourself if you've been willing to listen to the input of others weighing in about your child's needs. Their perspective may be valuable (although it isn't always), so be prepared to listen and willing to pivot if the situation calls for it. Even if you end up sticking to your guns, it's better to do so once you've been fully informed and considered the different options on the table.

The summer before Ethan entered kindergarten, I decided to write a letter to the school's principal. Although my parents had never intervened in advance on my behalf, I convinced myself that times were different, and I wanted to avoid having anyone rush to judgment about Ethan. In the letter I explained to the principal that, like me, Ethan was born with only one finger on each hand. I thought it would be informative and constructive to carefully describe his physical difference. I also explained that they could expect him to maneuver well in class, at recess, or quite frankly anywhere at school without any extra intervention. It never occurred to me to hold off writing the letter and simply ask for a meeting to talk about his abilities and receive their input first.

To my dismay, my correspondence completely backfired. In fact, it prompted the principal to request a meeting to discuss Ethan and what his specific special needs would be so the school could best prepare for his arrival. I was frustrated that my effort to avoid any fuss around his enrollment had had the opposite effect, and I turned to John.

"Why should we go? You and I both know that he doesn't need any extra help. I didn't need it, so why would he?"

My husband looked at me with his eyebrows raised, and reluctantly, I acquiesced. A few weeks before school started, I found myself at the meeting with the faculty, inwardly grinding my teeth as I listened to the principal.

"Mr. and Mrs. Zucker, the 504 plan is available to Ethan, given his disability."

Noting my hesitation, she added, "Mrs. Zucker, you wouldn't believe how many parents would give anything to have their child on a 504 plan."

The guidance counselor piped in, "We can work together to develop the plan so it is tailored to Ethan's needs. For example, if you'd like, we can let Ethan take all his tests untimed to make sure he has the time he needs to complete each in-class assignment and exam."

I responded, "Don't you all see? If you give him extra time on his tests, he'll take it."

I knew I was absolutely right on that point and continued, "He doesn't need the extra time now, but if you do this, he'll always think he does."

By the end of the meeting and after some private negotiation with John, I agreed to a modified plan, despite my better judgment. Essentially, the gym teacher would share in advance her lesson plan for the semester, giving me ample opportunity to show Ethan how to physically approach any challenges he might face in gym class.

Later that evening, as Ethan and I practiced stacking red plastic cups together in his bedroom, an activity the grade was scheduled to focus on that fall, I couldn't help but feel the faculty didn't really get it. I wished they had a true sense of our day-to-day experience, because only then would they understand Ethan didn't need, and wouldn't benefit from, their extra attention.

But in the end, a couple of the activities the gym teacher had suggested that we practice in advance actually *did* help Ethan participate at school with more confidence than he might have otherwise. I was ashamed of my behavior.

In the third grade, after Ethan had played soccer with the YMCA for a year, I decided to sign him up for a travel soccer league. Several boys Ethan knew from nursery school had already joined, but when Ethan was assigned to a team, I was frustrated that he didn't know any of the kids. Aching to have our son join a team where the kids were familiar with him, I phoned the head coach and told him, "Ethan loves to play soccer, but if you place him on a team with kids he doesn't know, it will disrupt his season."

The coach attempted to explain: "Mrs. Zucker, I know it's nice to have friends on a team, but those other boys are already showing signs of strong athletic ability. I think your son would be best on a team with children at his level."

I insisted anyway, convinced I knew what was best for Ethan.

The following week, my plan seemed to work. Ethan joined his friends on Team Germany, and practice went well. During the first game, however, he was mainly on the sidelines. After halftime he was put in to play defense for about five minutes, but when the opposing team got past him and scored, Ethan was called out again. Team Germany won and would remain undefeated that season, but Ethan's playing time and contributions seemed more and more irrelevant.

The weekend after the season ended, the league held tryouts to test ability for the following fall. The next morning, when teams were posted, I truly believe my heart stopped when I realized Ethan hadn't made any team. They also cut two other boys who had been similarly benched much of the season. I was furious. What kind of people cut an eight-year-old boy? But in truth, my rage was mainly triggered by guilt. Had I not tried to make things work out for him socially and listened to the advice of the coach, Ethan would have played more and perhaps developed skills on a team better suited to him. He also could have benefited from branching out and getting to know other kids.

These experiences forced me to take a breath. I needed to accept that while my motherly instincts were typically on the money, perhaps I wouldn't always know what was best for our child. Just as I felt emphatic that people get where I was coming from as Ethan's mother, it was also possible that someone else might offer something useful. As Ethan's biggest champion, I needed to be more open-minded to suggestions from others. Let go and let live also meant that I didn't always have all the answers.

EVERYONE WINS
WHEN YOU LET GO AND LET LIVE

Make no mistake. When you find the courage to let go and let live, your child isn't the only one who reaps the benefits of this important parenting approach. One of the most magnificent joys I've experienced is when I've braced myself, stood back, and allowed our kids to follow their dreams as I shared their delight in the process. Since nothing they are able to do is taken for granted, their accomplishments feel that much sweeter. And furthermore, they become a beacon of light not only to the entire family, but to others lucky enough to be touched by their strength, dedication, and perseverance. A great example of this is the story of Louie Edlund, as described by his parents, Theresa and Ryan.

Louie entered the world with a bang at thirty-five weeks. Born with a rare skin condition, he was rushed to the NICU for observation. At thirteen months old, he was diagnosed with trichothiodystrophy—a rare autosomal recessive genetic disorder. We read about what would come: immunocompromised, "wooly hair," short stature, bone abnormalities, feeding problems, and shortened life expectancy. The diagnosis confirmed what we knew in our hearts: Louie was very different. After several hospitalizations in the following years, significant regression and rehab needs followed, so we prioritized keeping germs away. Cleaning measures and isolation practices ensued, which felt valuable in the moment. We thought, if we can keep him healthy, we can make progress with everything else.

It was also during this time, however, that Louie found his love for baseball via the local Miracle League. The satisfaction and joy of seeing Louie happy were far too important to ignore because of illness threats. He looked forward to baseball night and bounced with anticipation.

The effervescence of Louie having fun had a ripple effect of smiles and laughs. We also became engaged in regular physical therapy where Louie learned to walk with assistance around the school—he was like a rock star and had to entertain his fans on his tours throughout the building. Everyone loved Lou for his very outgoing nature and charming smile. The social aspect and the fun were crucial for Louie to thrive and embrace what he loved. The balance of germs and adventure became a constant teeter-totter challenge.

Though it felt like we were providing for Louie in these moments, it became clear that the reverse was also true: Louie's life gave us life.

CHAPTER 4

A Helping Hand

At age ten I was in the bathroom at a relative's home when one of them knocked on the door.

"I'll be out in a second!" I shouted through the door.

"Hey, Meg, let me know if you need help wiping your butt."

When your child is different, and particularly when they're physically different, offers of help will be thrust upon them *all the time*, whether or not they desire it or need it. It's like living in a never-ending cartoon reel where Mighty Mouse takes the form of both loved ones and strangers who can't wait to come and save the day. Not surprisingly, most people will offer a kid help when their parent is not around. When you appear challenged, people continue to step in for the assist for decades.

You may simply feel grateful if people desire to help your child. After all, don't we all desire kindness for kindness's sake? Well, maybe not in every case. When your child is living in their own version of normal, the constant and often well-meaning attention can feel like an intrusion, like a bother-some seagull on the beach continually swooping in to intrude on your picnic lunch. Your child generally doesn't focus on being different unless someone else's actions force them to. And their reaction to offers of help is usually determined by a combination of their general disposition and their mood on any given day.

My brother Peter once competed in an Ironman competition in Florida. After he completed the race, I was incredibly impressed but also curious.

"Hey, P, what was the hardest part of the competition? The 2.4-mile swim in the ocean, the 118-mile bike ride, or running the 26.2 miles at the end?"

I figured he would tell me it was the final push—the marathon—after being exhausted by the back-to-back events. I was wrong.

"Meg, without a doubt, it was the swim. Trying relentlessly to push against the strong current was the worst."

Peter's words reminded me of one of the greatest ironies I experience. Despite the fact that I've spent years trying to resist the urge to interfere with our boys' independence, they still face an unstoppable stream of offered help. Being physically different means that when they go to a diner and reach for a glass of water, a stranger sitting nearby may suddenly emerge to help pick up their glass. Next, the waitress drops by and asks if they need a straw (despite the fact that they are already drinking out of their cup independently). Or, as they are replenishing from the pitcher left on the table, another guest at the diner rushes over to fill it up. The offers vary but have this in common—the experiences run counter to how our boys have been raised.

Similarly, your child may feel both patronized and resentful because of all the attention, especially as they grow older.

But here's the catch. While being on the receiving end of constant and unneeded offers of help can feel maddening, responding harshly to the well-meaning Samaritans can have an unintentional yet detrimental ripple effect. It's critical, therefore, to teach your child the lesson that took me forever to learn: It's okay to accept help, not because they need it but because others might.

THE DREADED INTRUSIONS

It's impossible for most to fathom how someone who is physically different can function easily and independently, so it is no wonder that people are compelled to help. In their minds, if the tables were turned, they'd be helpless. Ironically, I always joke that if, somehow, I miraculously grew eight additional fingers on my hands, I'd be a hot mess. What would I do with so many?

Of course, any young child is going to be assisted often by family, friends, teachers, and even strangers. They need it. The problem arises as they grow older. While other kids are beginning to function independently, your child who is different is developing at their own pace. The disparity is often the trigger that leads to those offers of help. The danger of accepting help, however, is that overreliance on others can further delay personal development. Understandably, your child might wonder, "Why make the extra effort to try if someone will do this for me?"

But as your child grows older and becomes more independent,

offers of assistance, especially if made in front of friends, can feel just plain humiliating. On one particularly memorable occasion, when I was eight years old, I so deeply resented someone for their effort to help me that I almost lost my sight in one eye trying to resist. I had planned to buy my mom pansies from a local store for Mother's Day. But as I approached the flower shop area, there weren't any pansies in sight. And worse, all the fresh flowers were in bunches and cost at least four dollars, more than my budget allowed. I then noticed a section of individual synthetic red roses in a display at the attached pharmacy. Desperate and with only minutes left, I glanced around to see if my dad was in sight. I then dashed over to the flower display and grabbed a felt petal rose with my small one-fingered hand. As I turned it upside down, trying to read the small price tag affixed to the wire stem, I heard the words I resented the most.

"Here, let me help you."

The offer was yet another reminder that the way others saw me was not the way I viewed myself. As the clerk reached for the stem to assist, I angrily pulled it back. He quickly lost his balance, tripping toward me. As I tried to escape his fall, I inadvertently thrust the flower's wire stem into my eye. In case you're wondering, whether you're different or not, the sensation of pulling a wire from your eye socket is neither desirable nor forgettable.

To give you an even clearer idea of what life is like when you're different, here are examples of the types of unsolicited offers I've experienced throughout my lifetime:

- "Hey, I can help you color." The boy grabs the pink crayon from my tiny hand (age 4).

- "Here, I'll cut the paper for you and make your snow-flake. Watch me." The girl takes my scissors and construction paper and sits at the desk next to me (age 6).

- "You must need help putting on your swim goggles." The swimming instructor snatches the plastic and thrusts them over my head (age 8).

- "Sit here. I'll let the teacher know you can't write as fast as we all can. Maybe you don't have to take the test!" a new friend says the first week of school (age 11).

- "Don't worry. I'll help you get out of it. I'll tell them to make you the manager of the team." A fellow student tries to help me, assuming I don't really want to try out for the girls' basketball team (age 13).

- "Don't worry, I got you." A stranger in the pool grips my bottom to thrust me out of the water after I just swam twenty laps (age 17).

- "Let me help you bring in everything. I can even unpack your things for you so you can relax," my college residential adviser tells me when I arrive freshman year (age 18).

- "The glasses can be slippery. Let me give you a straw for that drink," a waiter says as he serves me alcohol on my birthday (age 21).

- "Let me cut that up for you." A cafeteria employee seizes my knife directly out of my hands during my first year of law school (age 22).

- "We've taken the liberty of getting you a special computer, so you won't have to type," a partner at my summer law firm internship in Manhattan tells me, not knowing I've always been the fastest typist among my peers (age 24).

- "That must be so hard for you. Let me sign it." A fellow customer finds a pen to sign my receipt at checkout (age 27).

- "I'll put those on for you." A hotel manager enters the bridal suite and reaches for the earrings my grandmother gave to me on my wedding day (age 30).

- "Can I help remove your clothes?" a nurse asks during an annual checkup (age 33).

- "Let me do that for you." A stranger approaches me and my baby in a public restroom, picking up a diaper from my bag (age 34).

- "I'd be happy to help you remove your bra before you try on that swimsuit, if that's okay." A department store clerk enters my dressing room (age 38).

- "Here, I'll open that for you." A grocery store patron lunges for the plastic bag in my hands and begins to bag my apples (age 40).

- "No worries. I'll sign it for you." The UPS employee delivers a certified package requiring *my* signature (age 41).

° "I can do that for you." A man staying in the same hotel walks by and snaps up my key card as I am about to swipe it to get into my room (age 43).

° "Allow me . . ." The flight attendant on an airplane reaches for my seatbelt (age 46).

° "If you need me, I can help you when you come out." A stranger points to my pants and offers to buckle my jeans as I enter a stall in a public restroom (age 50).

Although these examples come from my own life, they aren't unique to someone who looks physically challenged. Once your child is mature enough to understand and reflect on their own feelings about these types of intrusions, consider periodically checking in and asking about their experiences. By making the effort, you'll gain valuable insight into the types of attention they loathe, so you'll be better equipped to lead them through and beyond it.

WHEN AND HOW TO ASK FOR HELP AND HOW TO RESPOND TO OFFERS OF HELP

One holiday break, John and I decided to drive down to the Outer Banks in North Carolina with our three kids. After a grueling daylong drive, we arrived late at night to the rental house. But just as we got there, we were greeted by a powerful rainstorm with multiple tornado warnings blasting from our collective cell phones. Trying to keep Ethan, Charlie, Savanna, and, quite frankly, ourselves calm, John and I shepherded everyone to the basement to play what every Jewish family does on Christmas Eve . . . a mean game of dreidel. As I watched Ethan masterfully spin the small, wooden, four-sided top with his own two fingers, I thought about how his Sunday school teachers had leapt to try to help him, assuming the maneuver was impossible. Because of our parenting style at home, Ethan knew he was fully capable, but struggled to confront any person of authority who tried to intervene.

With this in mind, I've thought about the word "relentless" in a couple of different contexts. On the one hand, there are the persistent strangers who relentlessly interject into your child's life with misplaced efforts to help. But the word "relentless" also describes your child's determination and commitment to assert their independence in the face of these intrusions. Yet there are also times when they realize they do need the help. In other words, it's complicated. It's your job, therefore, to have your child reflect on their own behavior and anticipate how they might best manage people's responses to them. Here are some examples to describe to your child as they encounter different scenarios:

- The Struggler, Type I: Your child is trying to physically handle something and is committed to success. They just want to be left alone to try. If someone approaches them and offers help, they can smile and refuse by telling the other person, "Thanks, but no thanks!"

- The Struggler, Type II: Your child is trying to physically handle something and is committed to success but realizes they can't accomplish that task on their own. They begin to look around, searching for someone to assist. Now they're ready to be offered help. If someone approaches to help them, your child should thank them with sincerity.

○ The Asker, Type I: Your child is trying to do something but immediately realizes they need help and is motivated to ask for it. On balance, they're sacrificing pride for practicality. Teach them that this realization is not a weakness but in fact a strength. Explain to them that everyone in the world asks for help when they need it—not only people who are different.

○ The Asker, Type II: Your child needs help, but it's hard for them to admit it. If someone (safe) approaches them to help, tell them it's completely normal to accept it. They might also be put in a position to help other people, too, someday.

○ The Leaver: Your child tries to manage on their own but fails. For example, maybe they attempted to open a plastic bag of chips, only to shove it back into their backpack unopened, embarrassed and unwilling to seek help. Maybe they're tired that day or feel overly self-conscious, so their pride is particularly fragile. They might want to be left alone and leave the scene before someone can offer to help. Let them know that leaving is okay, and they should never feel forced to ask for help if it doesn't make them feel good inside.

- **The Patronized Type:** Someone rushes to help your child and doesn't give them a chance to decline the offer. They feel belittled. If they are younger or the undesired help comes from an authority figure such as a teacher, your child may feel like they have no choice but to accept it. Tell them it's okay to let people know they don't need help, even people with authority. Teach your child to graciously decline if the offered help was not needed, knowing that they've educated their teacher about something they didn't know!

- **The Conversationalist:** Your child needs help with something but their modus operandi is to come at it indirectly, perhaps having an innocuous chat with another person before asking for help. A reference to something unrelated that happened at school or even about the weather could be followed by "Oh, would you mind helping me zip up my coat?" Let them know that this approach is totally fine and can make everyone feel more comfortable.

- **The Jokester:** Your child feels awkward asking for help. They might try to joke around a bit at first, perhaps using self-deprecating humor or being super silly about the task at hand. Tell them this is totally fine. It lightens the mood and can lay the groundwork for building courage to ask for the help they truly need. Let them know, however, that not everyone will be ready to appreciate their comedic approach, and if not, consider the route of the Conversationalist as a Plan B.

- The Praying Mantis: Watch out! A well-meaning offer of help can get someone's head bitten off. Share with your child that this type of behavior doesn't help anyone. If unsolicited help triggers inner rage, remind them that an angry outburst is never the right response to someone who acted with the best of intentions.

At this point I need to confess that I have behaved bitingly and harshly to well-meaning offers of help more times than I care to remember. And not just when I was in a particularly sour mood or when I was low on my dignity ladder. I've been a Praying Mantis many times over the course of my life. If someone were to observe me without intervening, they'd often take me for a Struggler, Type I. But instead of being left to do my thing, I'm frequently offered help. And instead of responding with a gracious "No, thank you," an inner rage has, at times, emerged. It's as if I were Bruce Banner transforming into the Hulk without any warning. I've gone into Praying Mantis mode at Starbucks, giving the evil eye to the barista who helped me place the cardboard sleeve around the cup before I could do it myself. One day I was so resentful that I removed the sleeve, only to put it back on myself to make a point. And then I fumbled a bit, and the coffee spilled onto my own sleeve. On another occasion, a man who happened to be in line behind me at the grocery store sweetly offered to put food on the conveyor belt for me. I was beyond perturbed and mockingly replied, "Why? Do you need me to help *you* put your own food on it?"

I know I left him shocked and no doubt regretting he'd opened his mouth. I had not even considered that he might withhold a similar offer in the future to someone who could really have used the help. I'm not proud to admit that.

Another evening at a Japanese restaurant, I was picking up a piece of toro sushi. I had spent years figuring out how to use chopsticks so I could function like everyone else at my table. And then, a poor schmuck (the waiter) met my wrath after he offered to give me a fork. The same scene had played out the prior month at the same restaurant (different schmuck). If I were the star of the sequel of my own horror movie, it easily would have been called *The Praying Mantis Returns*.

These examples are just the tip of the iceberg, I'm afraid. I used to bark at the conductor who took one look at me and gave me a discounted train ticket. Holding on to my pride, I'd insist on paying full price no matter what. I was so angry, that their intentions meant nothing. To me, it was an insult. Why would I deserve special treatment? I had no challenges getting on a train. Thankfully, over time (and after many discounted rates offered and declined), I came to an alternate solution. Why not pay it forward? Now, whenever I am offered a discounted price because of how I look, I no longer feel resentful. I've put my Praying Mantis into deep hibernation. Instead, I am grateful to be in the position that I can accept the cheaper rate and pass the savings on to the first homeless person I encounter or another charitable opportunity.

One evening, while discussing with my kids one of our recent encounters with an overzealous do-gooder, I decided to 'fess up about my prior anger issues and make it a teachable moment.

"I want you to know I'm ashamed that sometimes I've lashed out when people tried to help me. I was selfishly thinking about myself and how I didn't need the help. But in doing so, I likely blocked them from being nice to the next person. If offering help makes someone feel good, then they will do it again and maybe for someone who actually needs it. We just need to let them. It's just like when we want to do something to help others, too, since it feels so good."

I also discussed the Butterfly Effect with my kids. Essentially, any time we are offered help we don't need, we should remind ourselves that an angry or resentful response can have a negative ripple effect, changing other people's behaviors in the future.

The next morning, I swung by the grocery store with Charlie by my side. As I reached for a plastic bag to fill with a few apples, a fellow customer offered the inevitable "Hey, need some help with that?"

I glanced at Charlie, seeing his face strained—his pride directly joined with mine. I had to avoid another negative outburst in a grocery store.

"No, but thanks so much. I really appreciate it!"

The man at the store and I both smiled, and he wished me a good day and went his way. I was finally walking the walk.

This makes me realize there is another type missing from my prior list of expected behaviors:

○ **The Motivator Type:** Instead of being silently bitter or outwardly resentful at the unnecessary offers, help your child appreciate that just by being themselves, they have motivated someone else to be kind to them and, we can hope, to others afterward.

Oh, and for the record, I no longer use chopsticks. What was I possibly thinking? It is undeniably easier for me to use a fork. These days, waiters just smile when handing me a utensil, often unprompted. And now I swallow my pride, gratefully accepting their genuine offers of help. Let's face it. I'd be the real schmuck if I decided to decline.

INVITE YOUR CHILD TO SHARE THEIR PERSPECTIVE WITH YOU

It is hard for most people to imagine a life in which they're immediately perceived as less-than by everyone around them. And although I can offer insight into different ways your child might navigate well-meaning interventions into their life, each child really needs their own tailored plan that reflects their unique experience. I am reminded of a father who was trying to teach his legally blind son how to safely cross the street. But every time this dad would take a step back to encourage his son to cross by himself, someone would invariably grab the boy by the elbow from behind. The father was so focused on training his son to be safe that he hadn't considered what it felt like to be in his son's shoes. The boy became frustrated, telling his dad he wanted to go home.

"You don't understand what it's like!" he shouted.

But the father desperately wanted to understand. Asking his son to sit on a bench for a moment, he grabbed his son's walking stick and pretended to cross the street. On three separate occasions, strangers grabbed his arm from behind to help.

"I was startled every time they touched me . . . and became increasingly annoyed," he said.

Your child desperately needs to know you get it. By taking opportunities to understand their experience and listening to them describe how others' reactions make them feel, you'll be better equipped to support them in meaningful ways. If you can't witness what they're going through directly, ask your child to provide you with their own examples. Consider role-playing and reverse role-playing each scenario, pretending to be them and vice versa. Ask questions like:

○ How did it make you feel when someone offered you help that you needed?

○ How did it make you feel when someone offered you help that you didn't need?

○ How does it make you feel when you help me with something?

○ What might you have said to the stranger rushing to help? How can you respond the next time it happens?

See if you can answer the same questions for yourself. Consider going first. That way, you can describe how you felt experiencing each encounter. But be sure to give your child a chance to share how it *really* feels to be them. Come up with ways to react and respond that feel right. When you engage in dialogue, your child gets a chance to enlighten you as you grow closer to each other in the process.

LEARNING TO SWALLOW YOUR PRIDE

I recall an old saying by a nineteenth-century rabbi named Yosef Yozel Horowitz: "Man should control his pride. If not, his pride will control him."

I cannot decide what has been harder: helping our boys build their sense of self, or showing them when they need to swallow their pride. While the former is all about them, the latter is also important for the benefit of all. As I've suggested, a child who is different may need to let go of their ego when offered help they don't need.

So how do we help them accept unnecessary assistance without simultaneously destroying their dignity?

My mind leaps back to Tony Memmel who, thanks to his amazing parents Katie and Todd, grew up to become an accomplished musician, teacher, and global disability advocate. Despite his success, Tony continually gets confronted by people who insist on helping him. He describes one instance when he was performing in Johor Bahru, Malaysia, in front of a crowd of thousands, all about to be electrified by his talent:

The roar of the audience was deafening as the final chord from my guitar rang out in the filled-to-capacity auditorium, concluding the most frenetic concert I've ever played. Striking a Springsteen-esque pose, I raised my left arm into the air. At the end of my arm, near my elbow, the shiny, black, homemade industrial-duct-tape cast I use to play guitar, dripped with sweat. I waved it as both a "thank you" to the screaming crowd, and as my unspoken encouragement to the audience that anything is possible in life.

Early the next morning, I was still sailing on the adrenaline rush from the concert as I went to the hotel lobby for a big buffet-style breakfast. As I walked through the room, trying to decide which warm breads, local fruits, steaming noodles, and juicy meats to pile onto my plate, a waiter noticed my hand difference and approached me.

He insisted on helping me through the buffet by holding the plate himself, and scooping food for me. "Thank you, sir," I said, "but I can do that myself." He kindly refused my protests and persisted by taking my plate away, acting as an unrequested escort.

There I stood: a professional, touring guitarist, speaking to crowds every day about capability over disability, being shepherded, item by item, through a breakfast line like a toddler.

I'm an experienced traveler who has adapted ways of carrying my own suitcase, guitar, backpack, and a hot cup of coffee through airports, seaports, and cities around the globe. I did not need "help" with my breakfast plate, and at first felt silly about his attention to me. I prefer a person's attention to be on my music and message, not on mundane tasks I've been doing all my life.

My parents instilled this healthy spirit of determination and independence in me, and it has been a solid foundation in my life. From my first scoots on a linoleum floor learning to crawl, to chores, to interactions with kids on the playground, to varsity sports, to practicing music, my mom and dad expected that I would be responsible for myself. The encounter with the waiter brought to light another important life skill my folks taught me: humility. They ingrained in me that the Jedi-style move when I encounter someone like that "helpful" waiter is for me to be self-aware and confident enough in my abilities that I can put my pride aside and accept help from others with humble appreciation.

What I love the most about Tony's story is not only that his parents encouraged him to be self-reliant, but also that they made sure he was self-aware. In other words, he'd been raised to feel secure about his abilities. So when the waiter kept insisting on helping Tony, he was able to face the encounter with confidence. When you truly feel self-assured in your capabilities, offers of help don't tend to weigh on you. It's almost like winking at yourself and thinking, "I got this," and so the external noise doesn't matter. Tony was able to get through this and similar experiences and still land strong because he conducts himself by embodying my favorite mantra: "What you think of me is none of my business." People's thoughts and actions don't serve as a measure of your worth.

Tony also spoke of the value of humility, which is freedom from pride, subsuming one's own ego. Humility is also often considered the ideal way to accept an honor. One minimizes one's own importance in order to elevate another. It's a generous act. And that got me thinking: if a person's intention is to bestow something wonderful toward you (offering help), then the humble and generous response is to appreciate that the other person is actually just trying to honor you in their own way. This perspective makes it so much easier to graciously accept or reject their offer of help.

We can take that lesson to our kids and provide them opportunities to understand how magnificent it feels to help another. Then they will better comprehend what is motivating so many people to help them. One Christmas Eve, our family volunteered at a nearby church and brought food and toys to families in need. It's interesting to me that after all these years of giving gifts to our kids for the holidays, this memory is one they repeatedly bring up with fondness.

It might also help to explain to your child that pride can be a factor in someone else's decision to help. Once when I was visiting my maternal grandparents in Yonkers, New York, I decided to accompany my grandfather Ozzie to the grocery store to buy a few things. As we turned to leave, I tried to carry one of the bags, but my grandfather noticed a few adults around his age also leaving the store staring at us.

"C'mon, Grandpa! Let me . . ."

I grabbed the paper bags from his hands. The other patrons raised their eyebrows, judging him. How dare he let me, a girl with only one finger on each hand, carry our bags.

"Absolutely not!" he barked.

Immediately, with one hand, he grabbed the bags back, and with the other, grabbed my arm as we walked to his car in the parking lot. I was devastated. Couldn't my own grandfather at least understand that I didn't need his help? I was too young to realize that his actions had nothing to do with my pride but his own.

OFFERS OF HELP CAN ALSO BE APPRECIATED

Sometimes offers of help are the very thing a child needs, and the benefits can flow in many directions. Jen Gottlieb's son Cole was born with cerebral palsy, and Jen describes how grateful they feel that people try to help Cole:

Cole has a speech impairment, orthopedic impairment, and ongoing issues with his motor control. Multiple therapies are crucial in helping with these challenges. For example, Cole did not take any steps toward walking until he was four years old; these steps were taken in an assistive gait trainer/walker. He needs assistance throughout the day with tasks that many of us take for granted. Cole has a wheelchair, gait trainer, and other pieces of durable medical equipment to help him with his mobility.

Cole starting school was a big concern to me and my husband, Adam. Honestly, we did not know how other children would treat him. Cole attended a public school in a self-contained classroom for kindergarten and first grade; it was a class for children with speech impairments. For second grade, Cole entered the "mainstream," and he had to transfer to the public elementary school in our designated school zone. We did this with a heavy heart. I had been a substitute teacher at Cole's previous public school, and I'd gotten to know the staff and students there. My intention was to work at Cole's new school, certain it would benefit both my son and me. Cole received a one-on-one paraprofessional who would help throughout his day. We felt terrified with anxiety knowing that Cole would be one of the only differently abled students with an orthopedic impairment at his new school. The principal and staff assured us, however, that they would do their best to make it a smooth transition for Cole, and he would be well taken care of.

Cole started second grade at his new school in the fall, and our fears decreased when he was assigned a terrific teacher, and the students really seemed to accept him. One of Cole's new classmates was another teacher's son, who turned out to be a close friend, along with a few others. That became a true gift to us since the assistant principal told me that the boy created a game he and other kids could play with Cole at recess.

As a substitute teacher at Cole's school, I was able to meet many students, and I got to see Cole in the halls with his classmates. I noticed that different students would help push his walker to recess so he could switch to his walker from his wheelchair to play outside. I came to find out that the teachers had made it one of the weekly student jobs. Yes, a student would pick the job of pushing Cole's walker! Cole's paraprofessional informed me that some students really wanted this job because they wanted to help Cole. This made Adam and me feel so happy that Cole's classmates could be so caring.

When Cole was in fifth grade, his teacher and the other students were committed to making Cole feel like he was one of them and helping him in any way he needed.

One day, when the students had to pick partners for a project, several raised their hands to work with Cole. I held back my tears when I heard this. Helping Cole had as much of a positive effect on the other students as it did for him. We knew we made the right decision to have Cole transition into a general education classroom at that school.

Cole is completely appreciative of anyone who offers him help. It has also motivated him to help others whenever he can, and that means so much to him, too. Even when a total stranger at a Walmart store ran out to his car in the pouring rain to get a big umbrella to help us to our van, I thought, do people really do this? The man looked like our Uncle Jimmy from New York, and that made it even more special! When people are kind or helpful, it can be easy for some to look at this as pity. We choose to go in a more positive direction, and so we see this as compassion.

The reality is that although you may do everything conceivable to elevate your child to their greatest level of physical independence while helping them swallow their pride, there will still be things they simply cannot do on their own. But here's the thing. Just because they need the assistance doesn't mean it's easy for them to ask for or accept the help. Nor is this a short-term challenge, either. Just recently, John and I were invited to a friend's house for a celebratory brunch, where we could help ourselves to quiche, bagels, salad, lox, and desserts. The place was packed, and John was off somewhere engrossed in a conversation with a friend, already sitting at a table eating his meal. But I was stuck since I couldn't physically hold my plate in one hand and scoop food with the other. I looked around and just couldn't bring myself to ask anyone nearby to load my plate. With my husband detained, I was forced to consider my options. I could've put food from each serving tray on the top clean plate stacked on all the others, but that route was not viable since too many people were coming to grab a new plate. My next hope was to put my plate in the space in between trays and then serve myself, even if it was a bit awkward. But the trays were crammed too tightly against one another on the table. Strike three. So I stood there frozen. I began to walk away, deciding that if John did not free up, I'd grab something at home later, but then one of my best friends saw me and intuitively took over. As she served herself, she handed me a plate and discreetly offered to put food on it for me. I was saved, no longer going hungry and beyond grateful.

This is but one example of many similar experiences throughout my life. Fiercely committed to being independent as a young girl, I couldn't bring myself to ask for help from anyone. If I couldn't open a carton of chocolate milk in the cafeteria at lunchtime, I'd eat my sandwich and be thirsty. If I was at my own birthday party and knew that a ribbon was wrapped too tight for me to pull off, I'd put the gift down until my mom could help me open it later. Even as an adult on a business trip, I'd prefer going hungry on a flight rather than ask the person seated next to me to help me open a bag of pretzels. The emotional challenge of needing help but purposefully refraining from asking for it reminds me of the pushmi-pullyu in the story of Dr. Dolittle. The pushmi-pullyu is a fictional animal that is a cross between a gazelle and a unicorn, with two heads on opposite ends of its body. When one end would pull, the other would struggle in the opposite direction.

For those of us who are presumed physically inferior at first sight, we spend a lifetime trying to prove ourselves. Therefore, the thought of asking for help can be excruciatingly hard; it defies how we wish others to see us and how we wish to see ourselves. I know that some parents try to reason with their children, saying things like "Hey, it's no big deal. We all need help sometimes."

But that is easier for someone to say when they aren't constantly confronted with people who jump to the conclusion that they are helpless because of their appearance. Speaking from experience, I can tell you that it's extraordinarily frustrating to feel that you are no better than a stranger's lowered expectations of you. It's like you've failed yourself.

Admittedly, this is why I kept pre-opening all those water bottles and chip bags for our boys when they were little. I couldn't stand the thought that they'd need to ask for or accept help, and I longed to preserve their dignity. But that wasn't fair to them. I've worked hard to let my children know that while I still grapple with this pushmi-pullyu internal dilemma, accepting any needed help doesn't make me or them any less of a person. It was such an important lesson that it deserved my repeating more than once as they grew older. Most important, if asking for or accepting needed help gets us closer to achieving a normal life experience while simultaneously motivating people to continue being kind, then we have helped both ourselves and countless others.

CHAPTER 5

What About the Rest of the Family?

recently heard a mixed-race person describe how she feels Black when she's out with white people and white when she's out with Black people. But at home? She just feels like herself. The description completely resonated. When a child is different, the daily challenge of fitting in is ever present. But on their own turf, they experience the comfort of family and familiarity. While they'll long for the same sense of normalcy outside the home, the valuable experiences they have with their family become a cornerstone in helping them be prepared for anything.

Regardless of whether or not a child is different, they'll learn early on that they can't get everything they want, especially if they have a sibling (including not just brothers and sisters, but also cousins or the like of a similar age with whom they spend a lot of time). But when you are different, siblings play a crucial, if unsung, role. Beyond the healthy development of family life that includes natural bickering among kids or the traditional team dynamics of kids versus parents, siblings provide a dry run of what to expect outside of the safe environment. Parents can't always be around. And even when they are around, they typically cannot offer the valuable perspective and street smarts of a sibling, let alone the mindset of a contemporary. That is because siblings tell it like it is: their comments, insults, criticisms, and kindness hint at what's to come from other peers, but from a safe space. Whatever bubbles up during the process, brothers and sisters are instrumental in helping a child develop a thicker skin when it comes to the comments of others they'll encounter. Most important, siblings show them they can recover. These special bonds at home become an important gift to all.

In my life, my connection to my brothers created a level of support I could never have attempted to orchestrate. Sure, sometimes we fought like cats and dogs, ratted each other out over stupid stuff, and otherwise couldn't stand one another in a given moment. But when it came to my physical difference and how I had to face the world, my siblings always had my back. I've also witnessed the importance of Savanna in both our sons' lives, particularly when they were little. It makes all the difference for a kid who is different.

LET NATURAL CURIOSITY GOVERN

There are many ways my parents instinctively refrained from overprotecting me. But until I became a mother to sons who both share my condition and a daughter who doesn't, I never appreciated how my mom and dad had a choice. They could have cautioned my brothers to go easy on me from an early age or called them out if they made a hurtful, insensitive, or ill-informed comment about me. This would have had the unintended yet harmful result that my brothers would have walked on eggshells around me to protect my feelings. Instead, by allowing my brothers' natural curiosity about my condition and abilities to naturally unfold, my parents helped our sibling relationship—and, in turn, me—to thrive.

I won't go so far as to say I actually enjoyed all the probing attention when it arose from my siblings. When I was a child, my younger brother Teddy loudly started asking about my hands and feet. To my frustration, his questioning happened without warning, no matter where we were. Some examples included:

- Out at the mall: "Daddy, why does she only have one finger on each hand?"

- While eating lunch at home: "Meggie, see, I have five fingers."

- At the swimming pool: "Mommy, why are her feet so small?"

- In the car watching me buckle my seatbelt: "How do you do that?"

One evening, when I was seven and Teddy four, we went to the Red Wheel, my favorite local restaurant in Champaign, Illinois. It wasn't the food that I cared about there, but the miniature wooden Ferris wheel, loaded with lollies for the taking, at the entrance. Within seconds of my reaching for a red lollipop, a task I could only accomplish by using both of my single fingers on each hand, Teddy blurted out:

"Why does Meggie have only one . . . ?"

Immediately, I wailed. He had interrupted my moment of joy, reminding me I was visibly imperfect. It was time for my parents to intervene—at least that was what I hoped they'd do.

"Daddy, Teddy is talking about my fingers again. Make him stop!"

But Ted's questions were certainly normal for any young child. I myself had asked my father something similar when I was in the bath at that age: "Okay, Daddy, now I understand why I only have one finger. But why do I only have one toe?"

But by the time the waitress arrived with our food, Teddy, Peter, and I were already giggling about nothing important. Although my brother Ted didn't realize it back then, he was preparing me for the inevitable comments that would be hurled repeatedly in my direction by other kids who were strangers. And although I didn't appreciate this in the moment, I deeply benefited from his natural curiosity.

Not only did I get the opportunity to practice my go-to responses with him, sometimes I practiced my distraction method on him, too. For every outburst of "Why do your fingers look like that?" I'd respond with something along the lines of, "'Cuz I was born this way. . . . Hey, Teddy, I love your toy truck! Did Grandma get you that?"

And so, just like lifting weights repeatedly builds up a muscle, Teddy's questions about my difference provided me with the necessary experience and strength to face future inquisitive children. And witnessing how he'd quickly move on also gave me special insight. If I responded to other kids by repeating the same answer, they'd get bored. And even if they came back asking the same or similar questions moments later, that day or the next, I knew I could get them to move on eventually, just like I could at home. This would not have been possible without our family's let-go-and-let-live philosophy that held my parents back from interfering.

Decades later with my own kids, I knew I needed to emulate my parents' approach when it came to Savanna's questions. One day when we were at breakfast and Ethan was eating a bowl of cereal, Savanna, age four, blurted out to her brother, "Why do you hold your spoon so weird like that?"

Ethan had to wrap his finger in a way that gave him enough grip so the spoon wouldn't slip from his tiny hand. Immediately, Ethan began to complain. "Mom! Tell her . . ."

I could completely relate but stopped myself from interfering. As much as I felt strongly compelled to scold our daughter or tell her to back off, I remembered how my parents supported my own development by holding back.

"Well, E, explain it to her."

And so he did.

SIBLING RELATIONSHIPS ARE A GIFT

Parents are understandably trying to anticipate, manage, and maneuver every emotional and physical interaction for their child who is different. It's so easy to be consumed daily with reservations and anxieties like:

- Should I have done X for him?

- Shouldn't I have tried Y for her?

- Have I done enough?

- Should I have done more?

- Are they going to be unhappy because of me?

While you are wrestling with these questions, siblings aren't caught up with those uncertainties. They're just interacting naturally with their brother or sister without automatically thinking about their difference as a challenge or complication. Siblings accept each other for who they are since they've never known anything different. This dynamic is a gift.

Monique Herrera described the importance of her younger son William's role when playing with his brother Matthew, who is legally blind:

> With no health or developmental issues and an easygoing personality, William quickly brought our family a sense of balance. As toddlers, Matthew spoke for William, and William saw for Matthew. Being the older brother, Matthew would always answer for William when someone asked William a question. William helped Matthew better understand his environment. When Matthew asked, "What's on the other side of the monkey bars?" William would answer, "Swings." Next, Matthew would ask William to take him to the swings. Their relationship was natural, and to me, remarkable. William also helped us

better understand Matthew's visual deficiency. For example, until Matthew asked William about the monkey bars, we hadn't realized that Matthew couldn't see beyond them, and we'd thought that Matthew had stayed by the monkey bars because he preferred it.

All grown up now, my brother Ted shares some of his own memories that underscore the importance of sibling relationships.

My sister, Meg, may have had to struggle for much of her life to come to terms with her physical differences. When we were growing up, however, I was often unaware of what she was going through, and generally I just saw those differences as being uniquely hers, and a part of who she is.

As a matter of fact, I always thought her hands and feet were cute. We had names for them, and they actually had a lot of personality. Like any kid, I had various toys and stuffed animals, Legos, and so forth, but none of those things were as entertaining as the elaborate stories and plays Meg and I would act out with our hands as characters. As I recall, my fingers never had particularly distinct personalities; they usually played various bit parts, while her extroverted characters were the center of the drama. We had a lot of fun really.

And it's not as if she never struggled to accomplish something that would've required me or our brother to help her out. She just did some things differently. She could tie her shoelaces. Her handwriting was always a lot better than mine. These are things that no one else could have taught her; she had to figure out how to do them herself. Later I would come to appreciate just how tenacious and persevering Meg really is.

Except for a period when our family lived abroad, we lived in the university town of Urbana, Illinois, a two-and-a-half-hour drive south of Chicago. Perhaps the first time that I became aware of the difficulties Meg faced was when we made a family trip to Indiana. I didn't know why we were going there until we showed up at a very unpleasant place—I don't remember if it was a factory, but it had an unsettling industrial feeling, and I remember my sister was upset. This was where she was fitted for the orthopedic shoes that she would come to despise. These brown leather shoes were not made to flatter the wearer; in fact, they looked like they were designed for baby elephants to go bowling in. They had thick soles and were quite heavy— potentially deadly if thrown, which she did a couple of times when hard-pressed (like any siblings, Meg, our brother Peter, and I had our share of quarrels!).

Junior high school creates a challenging social dynamic for anyone, so it's not hard to imagine the issues my sister would face if she continued to wear the terrible shoes that she bitterly complained about but was told she must wear, lest she injure her feet. But Meg would not be deterred, and I remember how happy she seemed when she came home one day with a new pair of shoes that looked just like everyone else's. Sure, they fit differently, but they worked just fine. She must have learned to be thrifty, as she had to save up the money to buy them herself. The effect on her confidence was palpable.

My brother and sister became counselors at Interlochen summer arts camp in Traverse City, Michigan, where I was a camper. It was there that I saw Meg as not just an older sister—but as the role model that she seemed to have become for the cabin of campers under her supervision. She had a great rapport with these girls, and I could see that some of them really looked up to her for support and advice.

Other than noticing stares from others when they first encountered her, I really don't recall people treating Meg as someone to be feared or pitied. I'm sure it happened—like when we lived in the Middle East, where we found ourselves in societies where people with these sorts of differences can be marginalized. But overall it's worth noting how quickly people move beyond seeing Meg only in terms of her physical differences—I believe this is because she goes out of her way to be friendly and talk to people she encounters, and thereby sets the terms on which the interaction proceeds. If she were to act withdrawn and reserved, as many would expect her to, it would be different.

SIBLINGS OF A CHILD WHO IS DIFFERENT DESERVE TO BE PREPARED, TOO

Although you're understandably often focused on the needs of your child who is different, be mindful that their brothers and sisters also need your support. They, too, are dealing with constant questions about their sibling's difference, and it can feel like a torturous cross-examination. The interruptions can be blunt and often unexpected, including when you're not around to help them. In the same way I helped Ethan and Charlie understand why other kids might react inquisitively or even negatively, I similarly needed to prepare Savanna.

One morning she asked why kids kept staring at her brothers. I told her to imagine having a pet purple turtle. I explained to her that while we wouldn't think twice about its color, other kids who visited would want to ask all about it. In particular, they'd ask why its color was different from what they were used to seeing. Most important, I told Savanna that their curiosity was perfectly okay.

I realized the best way to help Savanna navigate others' curiosity was to forecast what was likely to come, in the same way I had for her brothers. I gave her a few examples of outbursts she might encounter:

- Why does your brother look like that?

- Ewwww! Why does he only have one finger?

- I'll be your friend, but your brother can't play with us.

- I bet your brother can't do that.

- Your brother looks weird.

- Why isn't your brother normal?

I also explained that Savanna should try the same go-to response her brothers used: "Because he was born this way."

But if it didn't seem to do the trick and the other kid kept pressing, it was fine to reply, "Just because . . ." and attempt to move on to other topics with them.

I also wanted to distinguish comments made to her about her brothers that were rooted in curiosity versus harmful intent. As their sibling, she needed to understand the distinction. So when another child said something about Ethan or Charlie that was intended to hurt or anger her, I gave her the license to say, "I don't care what you think," and leave. And if they made her truly uncomfortable, she could simply walk away without uttering a word. It was important for her to know that.

These scenarios, with all their possible permutations, can certainly seem daunting for a sibling to manage. But just like your child who is different, their siblings, too, will acquire strength and maturity beyond their years. To make sure Savanna was fully equipped for the inevitable encounters, I also wanted her to learn to empathize with her brothers' life experiences. While she often witnessed the surprised, curious, and sometimes negative reactions, that didn't mean she really understood what it felt like to be them. To further prepare her, we again role-played potential interactions. But this time, I modified the questions and had Savanna pretend to be the person who was different, while *I* was the probing kid:

- Why do *you* look like that?

- Ewwww! Why do *you* only have [fill in the blank]?

- I don't want *you* to play with us.

- I bet *you* can't do that!

◦ *You* look weird.

◦ Why aren't *you* normal?

By giving Savanna even a few moments to experience feeling what her siblings faced regularly, I was bringing her one step closer to authentically supporting them, a benefit to all.

Katherine Kanaaneh, a mom of three children, her oldest born with autism, shared a difficult moment she used to encourage empathy between siblings:

All three of my kids were in the car and we were driving to take my son Tim to summer school. His school is thirty miles away, so it is quite a drive through traffic. We were five minutes away from school when this happens:

Tim: "Go bathroom."

Me: "We are almost at school, buddy. Can you please wait a few minutes? There is no bathroom here."

He didn't say anything for a few seconds, and then he opened the door. Thankfully he didn't fling it open, he just opened it. I was shocked that he did that because he had never done anything like that before.

Me: "Close the door, Tim!"

Tim silently closed the door; however, a minute from school he peed in his pants right there in the car. He didn't say anything while he did it, but there was nothing I could do as I was driving and really was at a loss for words. He had peed in someone else's car a couple of times, but had never done this with my husband or me, and he never gave any indications as to why he did it. Because he had done this with someone else, I kept a Ziploc bag in my car that had paper towels and antibacterial hand spray. When we got to school, I took the Ziploc bag out and gave him the paper towels to wipe up the seat and told him to put the used paper towels into the bag to throw away. I then sprayed down the seat with the antibacterial spray.

I walked Tim to his classroom and explained to the teacher what had happened. When I returned to the car, my eyes started tearing up because I felt so frustrated and helpless—I didn't know why he did what he did, and I didn't know how to help him. But my role as a mom wasn't over. As we began to drive back home, Callia, age ten, said to me, "I'm mad at you."

"Now what," I thought.

"Why?" I asked her, while I tried desperately to keep my emotions in check and blink back tears.

"He just peed in our car and you didn't do anything about it; you're not even upset!" she shouted.

I explained to Callia that I was upset, but clearly her brother was going through something that we didn't understand; something was upsetting him.

I told her, "When you've had a bad day—maybe something happened at school—and you come home and in your anger, you slam the door harder than you intended, how would you like me to approach you? Would you like it if I started scolding you for slamming the door? Would that make you feel better? Or would you like me to check in with you and see what's going on?"

As I shared my perspective, Callia realized that when

she's unhappy about something, she looks for compassion and understanding from me. This is precisely what her brother needed from me, too. I knew that if I started scolding my son, it would just fuel whatever was upsetting him. He doesn't have much language to express himself, but you know your kid; I could see by the expression in Tim's eyes and on the rest of his face that he was upset. I didn't want him walking into school feeling more upset, so the only way I knew to diffuse the situation was to calmly have him clean up after himself.

Callia thought about what I said for a few minutes and said, "I get it."

THE TRUTH IS ALWAYS BEST . . . FOR SIBLINGS, TOO

One of the most important things my parents did for me was never try to paint an unrealistic picture of my life's reality. When I was seven, my father crushed my secret hope. I had always believed that by the time I was fifteen or something really old like that, eight additional digits would miraculously grow on my small, deformed hands, and eight additional toes on my two tiny feet. I would be perfect, just like my family and my friends—it was only a matter of time. One day I decided to share this fantasy with my brother Teddy, who received the news wide-eyed but circumspect. He rushed up to our father and told him what I had shared. But my parents knew better than to allow false hope to fester.

"Teddy, your sister is the same person you've always known. She's always had one finger on each hand and different feet and always will."

We both heard him loud and clear. Teddy took one more look at me and left to play with his toys. Forced to reckon with the fact that I would look this way forever, I cried myself to sleep. But my brother needed to hear it, too. Just as I was forced to face my own truth, it was essential that my siblings, who were around my age, needed to know what I knew—not more and not less. And the inverse was true. What a disaster it would have been if my parents had confided only in Peter and Ted information about me that they had learned from a doctor or specialist. Because my parents were always willing to honestly level-set with both me and my brothers, a stronger bond formed among us all. As my fiercest defenders and champions, my family was prepared to support me to the greatest degree as I forged ahead.

EMPOWER ALL YOUR CHILDREN BY USING CREATIVITY

When your children are little, encourage creative games that put them on a level playing field. Consider using the very thing that makes your child different as the basis of an activity that provides them freedom of expression and joy. Your child will feel empowered in this safe setting, and it can be fun for all involved.

When I was around seven, my brother Ted and I used to

watch *Mister Rogers' Neighborhood.* At some point during each segment, the neighborhood trolley would leave Mister Rogers's house through a tunnel into the Neighborhood of Make-Believe. Seeing how much we loved the show, my mom wanted to feed our imaginations and purchased Hansel and Gretel felt puppets for us to play with. In order to support their "heads" and "hands" for our imaginary play, however, I would need a minimum of three fingers and was stuck. Either I had to have Gretel's head flop downward as I used each finger to support her hands, or her head would be upright, but she couldn't move her arms to express herself. I was frustrated. When Teddy approached me again to play with the puppets, I refused.

"Okay, let's do something else!" he suggested.

But I sat on the family room couch and brooded. Reality would often bite at times like this, when I'd be reminded that the world wasn't built for the likes of someone like me. In fact, there was nothing more that I wanted to do than to play with the puppets. I confided why I was frustrated with Teddy, but he couldn't think of anything to say at that moment. Shedding a few tears, I began to play with my Barbie dolls until he returned with a pen.

"Here, give me your hands."

Ted then proceeded to draw two dots on the back of each of my minute hands and a half circle in each palm.

"Meggie, these dots are eyes and if you hang your fingers downward, it looks like each finger is a trunk."

He pointed to the half circle. "Oh, and this is their smile."

But he wasn't done.

"If you put your hand in the middle of my two hands, it

looks like my hands are the wings and your hand is a bird, flying!"

To this day, I'm not sure why we named my hands "Filet" and "Cutlet." But together, they were referred to as "The Birds," and when I turned my hands downward, "The Elephants."

"Hi, how have you been, Filet?"

Teddy looked directly at my hands, waiting for a response. I adjusted my voice to a higher and squeakier register and raised my hands up as if they were puppets.

"I am okay," Filet responded, sounding forlorn. "But the Momma Birds [my feet were cast in their own starring role] are not letting me or Cutlet come out and play."

To be clear, the Birds and the Elephants weren't exactly imaginary-friend material; it's not like I was ever alone in my room talking to myself. Rather, they represented freedom and equality to me when playing with my brother. Freedom because by using my hands during our version of pretend play, I was not limited by the design of an external puppet. Equality because the minute Ted and I ducked into our make-believe world, I no longer felt as if my difference made me "less-than." Playing these self-made characters with my brother reinforced my belief that I was just like everyone else. Actually, in some respects I felt even more special. Teddy thought Filet and Cutlet were spectacular, humorous, and entertaining. No matter what, they were always the stars, and I delighted in knowing only I was able to include them for our play. Once, after a particularly hilarious episode with my limb-inspired pals, he said to me, "Meggie, Cutlet and Filet are even funnier than you are!"

Strange as it was, he was right. It was because, in this context, I was experiencing the exuberance of being completely myself, channeling my personality through the very thing that had given me moments of shame in public. By introducing our private adventures with the Birds and Elephants and giving me the opportunity to unselfconsciously wave my hands and feet around in creative play as a very young child, Teddy gave me one of the greatest gifts of all.

THE BENEFITS FLOW BOTH WAYS

A child who is different isn't the only one to benefit from a sibling or peer family relationship. Their brothers and sisters become authentically empathetic and compassionate. It's also practically in their DNA to protect anyone facing adversity. I especially love how they gain a much richer and more mature perspective of their own lives and those they meet. When a child is different, their siblings tend to understand early on that there is much more to life than being popular or winning trophies.

At only four years old, Savanna began to demonstrate a protectiveness toward her brothers, staring down other kids who stared at them, as if she were saying, "You'd better back off!"

Savanna, now much older, recently informed me that she will still do that if she notices someone gawking at me or her brothers. Apparently, she waits until the other person catches her eye and then stares them down. Her goal? Mimic their glare until they are forced to look away. Yikes.

But that got me thinking. When someone looks directly at you, is your instinct to look away or meet the other's gaze? It has been well-established that sustained, direct eye contact is perceived as a powerful cue and can elicit fear in many species. In my youth, when other kids stared at me, often accompanied by a pointed finger, I would quickly avoid eye contact. Their behavior made me feel inferior, so I looked away. But averting my eyes signaled that I was giving up my own power. When I finally felt comfortable in my own skin years later, my go-to approach definitely improved. Now if someone gawks, I make sure my eyes meet theirs . . . accompanied with a smile. This simple gesture changes the overall dynamic from one of awkwardness to positivity. Sure, some respond with a smile in kind, while others become embarrassed that they've been caught in the act. But now *they* are the ones who look away. And most important, I feel like I'm back in control. It's a trick I've encouraged Ethan and Charlie to use, and I am now realizing it should be extended to siblings. Why not?

Because she grew up as their sister, Savanna became vigilant and motivated to enlighten others about her family. It would shape the type of compassionate person she'd become. When she was nine, she even joined me at an elementary school, the first of many events where we'd speak together throughout her childhood. After I shared a PowerPoint deck about our family with tons of photos, a fourth-grade student raised his hand.

"Everything must be so hard for Ethan and Charlie!"

Instantly Savanna grabbed the microphone and whispered to me, "Mom, I got this."

She turned confidently to the entire assembly of students in the auditorium, many of them older than she was.

"When people look at my family, they think, oh, it must be *so* hard for my mom and brothers. But really, my nut allergy is actually a hard part of our lives, too. A few years ago, the crossing guard at my school gave us Snickers around Easter time. They had pink Easter wrapping, so I had no idea what was inside. Charlie grabbed the wrapping after I took a bite and saw the ingredients included nuts. He screamed at our nanny while I went into anaphylactic shock and had to be rushed to the hospital! Don't think you know who is having a hard time just because of what they look like."

I beamed with pride and was impressed by the level of maturity and insight she had gained at such a young age.

Thinking back to Callia, I want to share her essay about her brother Tim, titled "My Brother Is Different and That's the Way I Like It," which won our nonprofit Don't Hide It, Flaunt It's first national Kids Flaunt essay contest. Callia's mom, Katherine, recently shared with me that because of growing up with Tim, Callia often demonstrates a deep level of empathy, understanding, maturity, and pride. Here is Callia's winning piece:

> My brother's name is Tim, short for Hatim. He has something called autism. Autism is something that makes it so he doesn't think like you or me. He doesn't talk like you or me. And I still love him, and nothing can change that.
>
> A nine-year-old girl like me might not want to flaunt something like this, but I can't keep my brother locked up so no one knows about him. I want him to SHINE BRIGHTLY! If you have a problem with that, then you try to take my place in the world! All I want is to have the

best for my big brother. I mean, he is twelve, and sooner or later he will grow up and I can't change that.

People treat me differently than others. Some treat me as if my brother is not so different from them. Those people are my true friends or just nice people. I've made friends and foes because of my brother. I'm flaunting this specific thing because I love my brother. I can't keep him a secret like he doesn't exist!

Beyond feeling protective, Callia demonstrated that she was proud of Tim and carried these lessons of acceptance and support of him outside the home.

Every April 10, siblings honor one another on National Siblings Day by posting photos of themselves and tagging one another on social media. One year I decided to celebrate the occasion by posting a photo of Peter, Ted, and me on my Facebook page. But as people from our past and present began to "like" the picture, I felt that the photo alone fell flat; it simply didn't do justice to the importance of our bond and their support of me throughout my life. This got me motivated!

As a result, Don't Hide It, Flaunt It (DHIFI) teamed up with Siblings with a Mission, an organization that provides support to siblings of those who have developmental disabilities and complex health conditions. Siblings with a Mission was started by Nathan Grant when he was in his teens, and he later expanded it while attending Harvard University.

Together, DHIFI and Siblings with a Mission provided a "Siblings Flaunt" platform for brothers and sisters of people who are different to share their own insights and perspectives.

I'm sharing here a few excerpts from essays written by siblings who participated:

- Six-year-old Connor wrote about his twin sister, Chloe, who is in a wheelchair and needs to use a ventilator to breathe: "I join Chloe at her doctor's appointments so I can hold her hand and say, 'You can do it!' My sister is brave!"

- Nine-year-old Grant McKay wrote about his brother Davis, who was born with Down syndrome: "Davis is different from a lot of my friends. He can't play the same games as me, but I still love him. I help him get dressed and help him play games that he can't play but I can."

- Teenager Cameron Reeves wrote about his younger sister Jordan, who was born with one hand: "While Jordan and I spend our time together bonding over music and video games, being her brother has been one of the best parts of my life. It's so amazing to be around someone who is so influential and inspiring."

Nathan, the founder of Siblings with a Mission, wrote his own "Siblings Flaunt" essay about his brother Nik. It captures the complexities of his own journey as a brother to someone who is different, including Nathan's candor about feelings of shame, as well as the benefits of connecting with people sharing a similar experience:

Growing up, I was ashamed of my twin brother, Nik. I was reluctant to speak about him with others. I tried to keep him hidden. Nik has a rare degenerative condition called mucopolysaccharidosis (MPS) type II, also known as Hunter syndrome. Due to his condition, he suffers from recurrent ear infections, intense gastrointestinal complications, and debilitating pain. He is also nonverbal, has a severe intellectual disability, and requires continual assistance from others, which predominantly comes from my parents and me. Although many of my brother's medical symptoms have been feasible to manage at home, it has been very difficult to manage some of the disabling challenges that have occurred in the public and broader community.

My brother often makes loud vocalizations, exhibits stimming behaviors like hand flapping, and frequently requires a special needs stroller whenever we go out in public. Although it can be infuriating to maneuver Nik's large stroller in small, crowded, inaccessible places, this has not always been the most challenging aspect of leaving the house. Growing up, it was extremely challenging for me to go out in public with my brother because of the people who stared at him. I became furious whenever anyone stared at him, and I would often stare at them right back in resentment.

The public gaze made me feel like I was different in a bad, unfortunate way. I often wondered why my family had to be so unlike others. Why couldn't I be like my friends who had healthy siblings? To make matters worse, my parents neither discussed nor seemed to be visibly disturbed by the people who stared at my brother. That made me feel even more different. Furthermore, I could not speak with my parents about these emotions and concerns because I believed it would only create more problems for them, and there were enough problems already. At times it felt very lonely. It felt horrible.

While speaking with other siblings [in similar situations] would have helped me feel less lonely, there were very few resources and support groups available specifically for siblings when I was younger. To meet and connect with others who share similar experiences, during high school, I created Siblings with a Mission, now an international organization that provides support to siblings who have brothers and sisters with complex health conditions. Through our online story columns, chat forums, and conferences, I have been able to connect with many siblings from around the world. It has been extremely helpful to speak and exchange stories with other siblings who truly get it. While our experiences may be unique from those around us, we realize we are really not alone. Like me, they have struggled with people who stare and have also experienced similar feelings of embarrassment, anger, and loneliness. Being in a community of siblings gave me the courage to address these difficulties. Shortly after starting Siblings with a Mission, I gave a speech at my school assembly to explain and raise awareness of my brother's condition. This was the first time I spoke so openly about Nik's differences, and it was empowering. To my surprise, the students and teachers in the audience did not look disturbed or bothered, but rather appeared interested and intrigued to learn about my brother and our story. I had assumed for so long that everyone judged my brother, but I was discovering that was not the case. Some people are genuinely curious about him. Realizing that shame and anger are not always the best response, I have learned to embrace curiosity and help others understand MPS instead.

Over time, I have found that my brother's diagnosis does not define him. While Nik will never say he loves me, he can still show it through his smiles and kisses. Although he cannot live like other people his age, my brother still enjoys life. He loves eating apples, going for walks, and looking at children's books. While we will never converse about school, family, and life goals, I can still enjoy my brother's presence as we live life together.

In the midst of the challenges that come with my brother's condition, it can sometimes be difficult to remember the positive life lessons my brother has taught me. But one thing is certain. Despite all the pain and discomfort my brother has experienced, he never forgets to smile. No matter how difficult life can be, I just hope that I never forget to smile, too.

Because of Nik, I am an advocate for those with complex health conditions. I am a supporter of siblings like me. I am a brother. So while people may continue to stare, I am going to embrace my situation because the imperfections in life have blossomed into something rather perfect, and there is no reason to feel ashamed.

Just take a moment to reflect on each sentiment shared by siblings about their brother or sister. The depth of growth and understanding due to their experience at home is immeasurable.

THE OLDER SIBLING

Older siblings are both a normalizing force and a valuable source of encouragement. They will expect their brother or sister who is different to try new things, succeed and fail, and, if a new task seems insurmountable, they are often the source of inventive work-arounds. Kids often take suggestions from siblings better than from parents, anyway. Just as important, older siblings have limited patience for those times when a younger brother or sister is tempted to indulge in self-pity. That's not a bad thing. That's a taste of real life that we all need to get used to. Nevertheless, older siblings provide a safe space for children to test their abilities, knowing that an older brother or sister won't constantly question their difference. They already get it.

In my own family, just as Ted helped prepare me for constant and unwelcome attention by bombarding me with questions of his own, my older brother Peter's interactions with me were just as valuable for different reasons. Most of all, he presumed that I could do anything, or at least I should try. He'd say things like:

- "C'mon Meggie, it's not *that* cold out. Let's play basketball."

- "Here, take my old bike. When you learn how to ride, we can get ice cream at Baskin-Robbins."

- "Okay, you build the snowman's face, and I'll build the body. Teddy, go inside and get some carrots and Dad's scarf and hat. Next we'll build a fort."

° "Don't worry that there are three holes in the bowling ball. I usually just use one mainly anyway. Try it!"

Essentially, Peter treated me how I desperately longed to be treated—just like everyone else. And that meant that Peter and I also fought constantly, just as siblings do. Peter never considered anything beyond my ability, even if it was physically harder for me to achieve. The importance of never feeling less-than in my own home, thanks to my brothers, cannot be underscored enough. In a world where others regarded me differently than how I viewed myself, the normalcy I experienced at home gave me both hope and affirmation.

Despite my love for ballet dancing that stemmed from my experience learning from my mom at the international school in Pakistan, reality crushed my desire to pursue it further when I returned to Illinois as a teen. One day when I went to sign up for a ballet class after school, I learned that there was a mandatory requirement to wear pink ballet slippers. Back at home, Peter was practicing the trombone in our living room. When he stopped to take a break, I confided how heartbroken I was that I'd never be able to pursue dancing any further.

"I think I'd have an easier time hanging the slippers on my ears than fitting them on my feet," I sulked.

But instead of allowing me to give up on myself, Peter helped me to move forward and cleared the runway for me to try something new. I would come to learn and cherish Peter's favorite motto: "Fail fast, then pivot."

It meant that while I wouldn't be able to accomplish everything, it was important for me to take failure in stride. In

Greek, "Peter" means rock, and my brother provided the sturdy emotional support I needed growing up when my physical abilities couldn't keep up with my desires.

That day, as I confided in Peter, a new idea suddenly popped into his mind.

"Here, I have an extra mouthpiece. Try blowing through it. Your lips are going to feel a little numb at first."

Grateful, I got up from my chair and held the round, stainless steel mouthpiece with both fingers. Peter had already been playing the trombone for two years. We were also both well aware of the story of our grandfather Ozzie, who grew up in an orphanage and was not allowed to attend Juilliard to study trombone, despite having received a full scholarship there.

"Now purse your lips together and blow! And try not to spit," Peter advised.

After several attempts, I made a strange, loud sound. I couldn't contain my excitement.

"Do it again!" he encouraged me.

But then, after making more wounded cow sounds through the mouthpiece, now attached to his instrument, my heart sank. As hard as I tried to extend my small forearm, I just couldn't reach every position on the trombone's slide.

"P, my arm can't reach that far. I can only extend it to fourth position," I whined.

Refusing to give up on the plan, Peter called our parents down to hear me blow into the instrument. He then insisted that my dad drive us to the music store, where Peter pressed the store clerk to make a slide extension enabling me to successfully play the trombone. And that was that.

A few years later, when Peter and I were in the high school band together, our conductor, Mr. Brooks, decided on the spot to make us perform a piece we'd been rehearsing. I was the youngest and only girl among the trombonists. Furthermore, I was seated sixth out of six chairs, with Peter as principal trombonist in the band, having held first chair the entire fall. The night before Mr. Brooks's request, Peter had happened to go out with the rest of the trombonists to a party while I stayed at home to practice. And so, when it was my turn, I happened to be more prepared. Mr. Brooks tapped his conductor's wand onto a music stand, making a loud, crisp sound.

"Meg, move up to the first chair!"

We were all stunned—me most of all. When I switched chairs with Peter, he mouthed to me, "You're going to pay for this."

And then he winked and smiled at me. I grinned back with temporary pride, knowing full well I wasn't long for playing as principal trombonist of the concert band. By the following week, when Mr. Brooks moved us back to our original spots, Peter couldn't wait to rub it in.

"Ah, back where she belongs!"

All the trombonists, including my brother, snickered. I relished being treated like one of them. And that was the point. Peter always made me feel like I wasn't his sister who was different. I was simply his sister.

I also followed in Peter's footsteps to the University of Wisconsin. During my junior year, when Peter was getting ready to graduate, I interviewed and landed a spot on the Homecoming Court. Although I'd imagined it was just an opportunity to meet the state's governor and do community service, I soon discovered at a meeting that it was actually a position with a lot of public exposure. I would be expected to sit atop an open convertible and wave to crowds in a parade through the city of Madison. Then the procession would move to the football stadium, and the Homecoming Court would be positioned at the fifty-yard line during halftime in front of eighty thousand fans. Afraid of the massive public attention to my one-fingered hands, I dashed out of the meeting to find Peter.

"Just focus on how you feel when you're at home. When you don't care about anything. Just pretend the crowd is me or Ted, Mom, or Dad." He paused.

"Life is however you decide to look at it."

Older siblings can intuitively and continually set a child who is different up for success, whatever that might look like, without causing them to feel patronized in the process.

LISTEN TO THE SIBLINGS OF A CHILD WHO IS DIFFERENT

Sometimes we as parents feel like it is up to us alone to determine what might be best for our child. It's so easy to convince ourselves that even if we don't have all the answers, we bear all the responsibility for our child's success. Siblings have a unique perspective and are a valuable resource, however. They are their brother's or sister's advocates, too, and can often spot an alternative approach that will provide their sibling a new opportunity to succeed. Pay attention to their insights; they offer an important home-court advantage to your child's team.

For example, as much as I abhorred the humiliation of going to a retail shoe store and seeing the salespeople awkwardly look at me when the foot-measuring device proved pointless, I was convinced that clunky custom orthopedic shoes would prove far worse. But by the time I was eleven, it was clear that I was uncomfortable in conventional shoes, and they began to pose an actual danger. One afternoon when Peter and I were biking in the neighborhood, we started to cross a street as a car was approaching. My right shoe, which was too big for my foot, flew off and caused me to crash. The approaching car screeched to a halt to avoid slamming into me. Peter ran to get help from a neighbor, and after that incident, my parents ignored my pleas to continue wearing "normal" shoes. That weekend, we all piled into the family station wagon to drive across the border to Vincennes, Indiana. There, a shoemaker greeted me with a poorly masked look of sympathy. He then dipped each of my feet into clammy, wet plaster and looked up at my parents as the concoction began to dry and take on the unique shapes of my odd feet. The shoemaker beamed at me and said to my parents, "She's never had shoes that actually fit. She's gonna love 'em . . ."

I frowned and my father proceeded to ask questions about the shoemaking process.

A month later, two pairs of new, custom-made shoes arrived. Enough time had passed that I had begun to hope that my new shoes would look prettier than anything I'd ever worn. I even fantasized that they would make my feet appear normal.

But no such luck. When I opened the first box, a pair of brown orthopedic shoes, completely faithful to the form of both tiny feet, were presented in brown tissue paper, waiting for me to wear. Observing my sullen expression, my mom attempted to soften the blow.

"Hey, they're not that bad. Here, look!" She proceeded to open the second box and pointed. "The wine-colored ones are even nicer. You can wear those with a new dress that we'll buy you for your bat mitzvah next year."

I despised those shoes. Sure, they were more comfortable than anything I had ever worn, but the young fashion maven in me knew they were undeniably hideous. If I had traced a pencil around them on paper, I would've drawn a small circle.

"They look like moon boots! I will never wear them!" I yelled.

Ever the optimist, my father turned to me. "Meg, look at the bright side. These shoes are made with a special type of steel at the toe. It's like having your own secret strength."

I left their room in tears. Overhearing the exchange, Peter came to our parents' room and asked, "Does she really have to wear them?"

They nodded, and my dad suggested that Peter help distract me from my distress about wearing the new shoes. But my brother had other ideas. He intuitively knew that the best approach to help me accept the idea of wearing the shoes was not to change the topic but to face it head-on and embrace it. Ignoring my parents, Peter found me in my room, looking solemn. I couldn't imagine having to look like a freak in those abhorrent shoes. There was something quite ironic about that, of course. Most people who approached me would be staring at my different-looking limbs, rather than those shoes. But to me, the shoes made me look even more freakish and therefore made things even more unbearable. I motioned for him to go away, but Peter refused and sat next to me on my bed.

"Hey, I have a plan," he said. "Dad told me that there's steel in the front of your shoes . . . kinda like having Superman's strength!" Memories of when we were little kids running down to the family room in our superhero-inspired pj's to watch the animated series *Super Friends* immediately popped into my mind.

He added, "I think these shoes are going to be the best thing that ever happened to you."

Curious, I listened. The next day, although I felt self-conscious about wearing the brown "everyday" moon boots, I couldn't wait until recess. When we were finally let out of our sixth-grade classroom to play after lunch, I ran to the kick-soccer field to join the game. Usually on any given day, I'd only be able to kick the ball a couple of feet, someone would catch it, and I'd be out within seconds. My poor athleticism typically left me one of the last ones picked on a team. But today was different. When it was my turn, I used all of my might to lunge toward the rubber ball and give it the biggest kick.

A kid in the outfield yelled, "Holy crap, Meg. It's a homerun!"

"How did you do that?" another friend asked me after I had run around all the bases.

Everyone's mouths simultaneously gaped open wide. Just as Peter had predicted, the steel plate at the front of my shoe gave me an almost superpowered strike. In fact, I kicked the ball so far, it landed past the diamond and almost in the street. From

171

that day on, I would be regarded as one of the best kick-soccer players in my elementary school grade. Was I cheating, given the advantage of my shoes? Umm . . . maybe? But the experience represented something critical. My older brother helped me transform a miserable experience into one of triumph. As a result, my parents began to realize that while they couldn't always make things better for me, there were others in the family who cared about me and just might.

DON'T FORGET ABOUT THE SIBLINGS

Sometimes, a child who is different will receive the lion's share of a parent's time and attention. Strike a balance and find opportunities to enjoy activities solely with each of their siblings. It shouldn't be just a one-off activity. Regularly schedule time when they are your only priority. They need and deserve it. Also consider planning activities for them where they aren't around anyone else in the family (yourself included) and can escape the home environment and focus on themselves. For example, a friend whose son has Down syndrome reminded me how essential it was for her daughter to attend her own camp during the summer. As my friend described it, her daughter needed time to grow and experience life without the ongoing focus directed to her brother at home. When she returned at the end of the summer, she was rejuvenated and had gained a new sense of commitment to her family. Her mother described this well-deserved breather as a game changer.

Stella Scheier, one of my friend Mindy's children, wrote a

"Siblings Flaunt" essay as a teenager. Stella's honest portrayal of growing up with her brother, Oliver, shows what it feels like when your sibling takes up much of your parents' time and focus. The essay ultimately reveals how Stella learned to appreciate the experience and its value in her own life, however.

Oliver has exemplified perseverance, determination, and courage from the second he was born. As his older sibling, I was an example for him, and I was there for him no matter what he had to endure. My life has most likely been different than anyone else my age. Most sixteen-year-old girls do not know the feeling of having their younger brother endure an eight-hour surgery that was incredibly risky because of his decreased lung capacity. They don't understand how it feels to see your brother struggle with things that most people take for granted, like running or getting dressed. No one else understands the heartache I feel every time my brother trips and falls without knowing what caused him to do so. But these feelings not only changed me, they have made me stronger and more appreciative of things most others take for granted.

At the age of two, Oliver had a feeding tube in his nose because he needed extra nutrients in order for his body to develop. Changing his feeding tube is an unexplainable experience. My brother was put through excruciating pain. I was only four years old and had no choice but to sacrifice my feelings and only worry about how he was feeling. It became my job as his older sibling to figure out ways to distract Oliver during this process. For example, I would dance, sing, make jokes—I would try anything I could think of to take his mind off his pain. But on top of that, it was also my job to stay strong: stay strong while my brother was in pain, stay strong when my parents were gone with my brother at doctors' appointments, and stay strong no matter what happened.

It is not always easy to stay strong and positive. Oliver definitely takes priority and consumes a lot of my parents' time. At least one of my parents handles my brother's doctors' appointments or his needs, while I am left to manage on my own. Throughout my whole life, I have always struggled with this; I sometimes found myself to be jealous of all the attention my brother received and all the time my parents spent with him. In these moments, I found having a sibling with a disability to be a challenge; it is hard to constantly know that my brother's needs are put before mine. At a young age, I was forced to figure out a coping mechanism to deal with the jealousy I felt toward my brother. As I grew up and matured, I realized that my brother does not want this attention, he does not want to have my parents constantly focused on him, he does not want them to always have to take him to doctors' appointments, he does not want everything that comes with rigid spine muscular dystrophy (RSMD).

Everything that I have dealt with so far in my life, all the pain I have been through, all the hardships my family has overcome, make me who I am. Having a sibling with a disability is something that I would not trade for the world. Oliver is not like any boy, and the way he deals with everything in his life inspires me every day. Although some days have been harder than others, being the sibling of someone with a disability is the best thing that has happened to me. Oliver constantly makes me laugh, he cares more about family than anything else, and most important, he lives every day to its fullest.

I thought my primary priority for Savanna would be to schedule playdates, shuttle her to practice, attend sports games, and of course manage her severe nut allergy. Meanwhile, I believed it was her brothers who needed any extra moments I had available for my kids. And so, distracted by different priorities, John and I missed the signs that our daughter needed more attention. When Savanna was thirteen, a child psychiatrist diagnosed her with ADHD. After a few sessions and tests, the doctor asked us when we first noticed that Savanna had an executive functioning issue. I could hardly look into his eyes, or hers for that matter, feeling immeasurably guilty and embarrassed. We'd been so focused on making sure the boys were okay that it seemed we ignored every sign that Savanna had been struggling with symptoms related to ADHD. That evening she called me out on it.

"Seriously, Mom? Why did you think I begged for you to sign the approval form so I could sit on a balance ball seat in elementary school?"

Savanna had been a devoted gymnast, and I just figured she liked to bounce on it throughout the day for fun. In reality, the ball allows kids to burn off their nervous energy and manage their hyperactivity during classes. That moment was a wake-up call. Whoops. She deserved more from us.

Another thing to keep in mind is that sometimes siblings, particularly older ones, place substantial pressure on themselves to be perfect. Perhaps it's subconscious, but they desire to give their parents a break and not become an additional source of worry. Whether they are chasing academic excellence, popularity, or just the role of peacemaker at home, the pursuit of perfection generates emotional pressures that no kid can handle. In our home, I have found it necessary to remind *all* of my children that no one is perfect, and we have no expectations that they would be. They also needed to understand that perfection is not attainable, so it's a waste of anyone's time to try. I return to my favorite analogy from the film *Moonstruck*: "Snowflakes are perfect. The stars are perfect. Not us. Not us!"

THE REVELATION

There's a moment for every sibling of a child who is different when they start to get it. Their family is different. Their brother or sister has unique or demanding challenges, and as their sibling, they have a role to play in making this all work. In the beginning, the experience may be difficult—enduring stares or comments directed at their family member, feeling angry but unsure of how to respond. And for some kids, there's a social price to pay. Some struggle with whether to invite a friend home to play, out of concern that they might react unexpectedly or uncomfortably to that sibling with a difference. The brother or sister of a child who is different might be tempted to pre-warn their friend about the disability or difference, but then remember that pre-warning can generate more unnecessary fear and anticipation than it's worth.

Many of their friends don't share the same experience, and it is hard to confide in friends who don't relate. This is a gap that needs to be filled because they deserve to have peers who get it. It's time to be proactive! In the same way that it is important for your child who is different to find their community of similar peers, consider making introductions with their siblings, to the extent you've developed relationships with other parents whose child shares the same difference as yours. Or if no one comes to mind, research ways to make connections with other families with siblings who can relate. Relevant and safe social media groups that hold in-person gatherings are a really wonderful way to ignite new relationships. Most important, developing these friendships can offer another avenue of support and be beneficial for all involved.

When Savanna was little, she confided in me that a boy at Ethan's soccer game had noticed me, Ethan, and Charlie and had begun to make fun of us at her school.

"Mommy, he was so mean about the fact that you and Ethan and Charlie were born with different hands. He said you looked weird!"

I paused and gave her a hug. Later that evening, I wondered aloud to John how many times unbeknownst to me that my own brothers had defended me or endured thoughtless comments and countless stares directed my way.

I always hoped that our kids would love and support one another. But when your child is different, the importance of having sibling support is elevated. The benefits flow both ways because the experience growing up with a child who is different impacts their siblings' emotional growth and provides an appreciation of the most important priorities. Of course, there are no guarantees, but it is undeniable that the siblings' maturity level and ability to be empathetic is often light-years ahead of their peers'. I've had the pleasure of witnessing how Savanna not only adores her brothers but honors them. It is so easy for parents to be primarily consumed by the specific needs of their child who is different, but here's the revelation: While your devotion is essential, don't overlook the immense value of siblings as a critical component of the "Team [fill in your child's name]" equation. Siblings' unconditional support, unfiltered approach, and challenges, understanding, and acceptance create an even greater win for all. There is a Vietnamese proverb that says "Brothers and sisters are as close as hands and feet."

Indeed.

CHAPTER 6

Taking the Bull-y by the Horns

On the first day of first grade, our son Ethan was bullied. Since I'd never personally experienced such trauma despite our sharing the same genetic condition, I presumed he would go similarly unscathed. I was clearly mistaken. Up until then, I hadn't actually given a lot of thought to the idea that other kids might be purposefully cruel to him. I'd been less worried about mean kids than the question of whether children would be mature enough to ignore social pressures and accept him as their friend. It was so easy to fixate on the brutal possibility of his being alone. I am reminded of a *New York Times* op-ed by David Axelrod, a political campaign manager whose daughter Lauren was born with epilepsy. David hit the nail on the head when he said, "Lauren's seizures had been terrifying and painful. But her loneliness was absolutely heartbreaking. She longed for friendships."

While some kids like Ethan unfortunately will be the

subjects of torment, many, like our son Charlie, will luck out and escape such experiences. There are no guarantees for anyone.

Earlier that morning, before I woke up the kids for our morning routine and Ethan's first day, I was already feeling nervous. It did not escape me that the mere sight of Ethan would trigger tons of unwelcome attention. Needing to lean on someone reliably unemotional to help brace myself for the day, I called my father. Although he was scrambling to leave for a work-related trip to Pakistan, he took the call and dependably coaxed me past any feelings of worry to those of acceptance.

"Meg, sometimes you just have to trust that there are reasons things are meant to turn out one way or another. You can't control everything, but that doesn't have to be a bad thing."

Ever since Ethan's experience being bullied in elementary school, I've observed two distinct behaviors among kids. While all kids invariably will be puzzled by the sight of someone who looks atypical, the majority are able to move on quickly. Some, though, will choose a darker path. And so, my job was to teach my kids to expect curiosity but to be prepared for the worst. And if the worst happened and another child was intentionally mean? Be prepared to respond with something familiar: Pity them.

The following week, news broke of a devastating magnitude 6.4 earthquake in northern Pakistan. Thousands of people had been killed, and thousands more were missing. With my rusty Urdu, I trembled as I dialed the cell phone number my father had left me. Miraculously, the Northern Frontier minister answered after a few rings.

"*Assalamu alaikum.* My name is Meg, and my father is Marvin Weinbaum. I am sorry to call you unexpectedly, but we heard on the news there was a terrible earthquake. Do you know if he's okay?"

In that moment, my childhood flashed before my eyes. My father's undeniable strength was a key factor in my own accomplishments and parenting triumphs. I held my breath and heard him speak in a muffled voice for a moment.

"Ah, yes! Professor Weinbaum. He is here with me. I will put him on . . ."

I sat down, feeling numb.

"Dad?"

Of course, he began by reassuring *me* that everything was fine.

"Meg, I'm okay, but you'll never believe what happened. The frontier minister asked me if I'd like to join him to view the region from the air. Just as our helicopter left the ground, the earthquake struck. The helicopter saved us. It's just awful. . . . I think most died at once."

As I reflected on my father's close call, everything he and my mother had done to support me in my life, and my own child being targeted for being different, I thought about how unwelcome experiences are truly out of our control. But if kids are fortunate, they will have parents who are committed to helping them both anticipate and respond to life's twists and turns. Only then will they know precisely how to manage through every unforeseen challenge and persevere.

WHAT WE, AS PARENTS, ARE WORRIED ABOUT

American journalist Nick Gillespie wrote an article in *Reason* magazine called "How to Tell If You're Being Canceled." In the piece inspired by an interview with Jonathan Rauch, a senior fellow at the Brookings Institution, Gillespie says, "Canceling is about manipulating a social environment with a goal of isolating or intimidating; it's about making another person socially radioactive."

As a person who is different and also raising children born with my condition, I've thought a lot about the notion of cancel culture, but in a personal context. When someone is canceled, they are ostracized and shamed for their views or actions. But when your child is different, they can be canceled just for being themselves. I liken it to unwarranted social leprosy.

When Ethan was in nursery school at the age of two, kids were certainly inquisitive, as expected. After he'd offer our go-to "because I was born this way" response, he'd tell me how they'd sometimes press with more questions. Oh, how I longed for our boys to remain in the happy bubble of kumbaya days, surrounded by other innocent, unconditionally accepting two- and three-year-olds. But nothing he mentioned raised the alert level of my personal mom-o-meter. In fact, his classmates quickly moved on to the next game, and no one fixated on Ethan's one-fingered hands. What was mainly worrying me was whether they'd be open to being his friend.

By the age of four, Ethan was still young enough to simply enjoy orchestrated friendships. And so I purposefully befriended many mothers, even those with whom I had nothing in common, because I was determined to take advantage of any budding spark with kids that Ethan met in nursery school and to satisfy his yearning for companionship. To be clear, there are no guarantees that every parent is open to having their son or daughter befriend a child who is different. Sometimes I wondered about those kids who were always "too busy" for a play-date. Once after nursery school, our nanny Joan observed a boy in Ethan's school named Mickey, who always seemed outside of the social mix of the other kids.

"Meg, it's hard for me to watch. So many kids seem to be avoiding this boy. He never goes over to play at anyone else's house, either."

The following afternoon, I observed that most of the kids, including Ethan (thanks to me), were piling into one another's cars for playdates. The next day, we invited Mickey over for a playdate at our home. While Ethan and Mickey mainly played independently, his mom was so over-the-moon grateful for her son to be invited, she even sent us a gift basket of goodies. Shortly after the end of the school year, Mickey was diagnosed with autism, and their family moved to a different state. Since then, I have thought a lot about Mickey's mom. I could certainly relate to feeling a strong level of gratitude toward anyone who included our child. It hadn't occurred to me that Ethan, also different, could serve in his own humanitarian role, offering friendship and belonging to another child not readily accepted by his peers. Like me, Mickey's mom worked. But unlike me, she wasn't very social. I wondered if she would have been more successful in arranging playdates for her son if she'd spent time getting to know other parents. Would the others have been willing? Perhaps not all, but we only need a few.

When Ethan graduated from nursery school, I observed an obvious shift. I could no longer orchestrate playdates for him based on my own friendships. It would take a special kind of kid to have enough self-confidence to look past superficial differences, ignore peer pressure or other kids' comments, and reach out to someone not perceived as "normal." And Ethan was not naturally social and gregarious at first. I was well aware, therefore, that based on his disposition alone, the friendship climb would be steeper.

On the first day of kindergarten, all the students lined up outside in front of their teacher. As expected, I caught many of them staring at Ethan. These encounters were often the same— one would notice him, whisper, and sometimes point. The "news" would then spread like wildfire. For the record, depending on your own makeup, it can take every ounce of self-restraint to stand back when your child is the star of the staring show. Others' incessant interest in your child, though innocent, can be emotional and painful to watch. Crushed by being the only one not invited to senior prom? Heartbroken on Valentine's Day? Jilted by the person you thought was supposed to be "the one"? Experiencing those things for yourself doesn't compare to seeing your child experience emotional pain that is out of both their and your control. There's a saying that you're only as happy as your most unhappy child. I can attest to that.

Even as a person who is different and has passed on my own condition, I find it harder to watch my kids suffer as the objects of constant attention than to have experienced the same thing at their age. Admittedly, I'm embarrassed at how I've reacted in anger to some of these innocent, inquisitive kids. As an adult, I've given the evil eye to a five-year-old. Later on, feeling ashamed by my own behavior, I confessed the episode to John. Instead of trying to make me feel better, he shook his head incredulously.

"Meg, ya know, I could have easily been one of those little curious kids back in the day whispering to my friends about you, Ethan, or Charlie."

John is one of the kindest, most open-minded adults that I know. Kids grow up. Point well taken.

As time progressed, while other students still gawked in hallways, at least Ethan's classmates grew accustomed to his difference. But just like anyone else, Ethan craved friendship. One afternoon things started to look up. As he was getting in our car after school, an adorable boy, with olive-colored skin, light hair, and brown eyes, ran up to him.

"Hey Ethan, can you ask your mom if you can come to my house Friday after school? See ya tomorrow!"

"Sure! See ya, Trevor!"

Ethan smiled. It's hard to fully describe the sheer joy I felt, knowing I hadn't orchestrated the invitation. I felt my heart melt. It's no wonder Mickey's mom sent me a gift basket. I was so grateful that if Trevor had asked me to buy him the latest Wii console (the premiere video gaming station in those days), I would have dropped it off at his doorstep on the spot. Over time, Ethan and Trevor spent many afternoons and even weekend sleepovers together. Then a few other kids began to follow suit.

Here's the thing. Ultimately, all my initial fears about Ethan developing friendships in elementary school were for naught. Perhaps friends don't emerge in droves, but there are special, wonderful kids who are likely raised by accepting and inclusive parents and who eventually show up. They are to be cherished.

CURIOUS VERSUS CRUEL

It is worth reminding your child of the difference between insensitive comments and intentional verbal harm. The former feels like bullying, but the latter often actually is. If your child comes home from school and informs you that a peer has been cruel, you don't want to take any drastic steps such as contacting their teacher, the school principal, or another parent based on a misunderstanding. I'll admit that I've been in this kind of situation where I heard about an interaction solely from my child's point of view, got incredibly worked up, and almost jumped to a false conclusion.

Andrew Solomon, a professor at Columbia University Medical Center, said, "To be found grotesque is often to become grotesque; we fit other people's perceptions of us and grow into what they see." His observation reminded me how critical it was for our sons to break the barrier and try to show other kids that they are a some-one, not a some-thing based on their appearance. I recall the day I took Ethan to the YMCA for his first swim lesson. He had just completed kindergarten, and we wanted his swimming skills developed before we sent him off to an all-day summer camp.

"You are a monster!" yelled a six-year-old boy loudly, pointing.

His words instantly stung both of us. Ethan looked at the other child, who continued to point at him, and ran over to me as he burst into tears.

"He's a bully! I want to go home," Ethan begged.

The odd thing about the encounter was that the boys were actually laughing and joking together at the beginning of the swim lesson. There they were, two young boys bantering back and forth, laughing as another girl in the class wore her goggles upside down. And then the boy suddenly noticed and reacted. And then the whole class noticed. I watched as the boy's mom, who was sitting on the nearby bleachers, sprang into action. Her face was beet red.

"Riley! Say you're sorry right now!"

I have thought about that day for years, since this type of unwelcome outburst is inevitable when another kid doesn't view you as normal. My role as Ethan and Charlie's parent was to make sure they understood the concept of intent and motivation when it came to deciphering whether another child was actually being a bully. Bullies want to cause emotional or physical harm; their motivation is likely attributed to a personal unhappiness or self-loathing. The encounter at the YMCA was different. As we drove home, I turned to Ethan, who was still visibly upset.

"Honey, for the record, he wasn't actually trying to be mean to you. That boy was afraid of something he hadn't ever seen." And then it was time to validate Ethan.

"I know . . . What he said hurts."

Although Ethan didn't want to return to the Y for lessons,

I knew my role as his parent was to not give in to his fears, nor my own. Making him return to the scene of the incident felt counterintuitive but essential.

"E, you know how we always say we forget that we're different unless someone reminds us?"

He nodded.

"Well, that is because we are so used to ourselves. Give that kid a chance to get to know you. You'll see."

And just as I predicted, by the third swim lesson, Ethan and Riley were laughing together again; only this time they decided to put their goggles on upside down on their own faces.

My friend Mindy shared another story about her son, Oliver, born with RSMD, a type of muscular dystrophy. When he entered middle school, which took students from five elementary schools combined, he was once again faced with kids who were unfamiliar with his condition. On one of the first days of school, a student approached him.

"Why do you walk so weird?"

Feeling bullied and extremely angry, Oliver retorted, "Why are your eyebrows so bushy?"

When Oliver came home upset, Mindy used the incident as a teaching moment and discussed the concept of pure curiosity. Though Oliver's classmate had used a very poor choice of words, he was simply reacting to something he'd never seen before.

She then asked Oliver, "Well, did you respond to the boy's question? Did you say matter-of-factly, 'Because my muscles work differently than yours'?"

Mindy explained to Oliver that he had missed an opportunity to teach the boy about himself and satisfy his curiosity. They both knew this wouldn't be the last time Oliver was asked about his difference. So to prepare, Mindy role-played with Oliver. She pointed at him and used terms like "creepy," "strange," and even "disgusting." The next time it happened was several weeks later.

A boy stopped Oliver and asked, "Why can't you run?"

This time was different. Oliver was able to respond with the explanation he and his mom had worked on at home. Though the kid responded with pity rather than friendship, Mindy felt it was a win on multiple fronts. Oliver didn't perceive the interaction as being bullied, and he was able to answer the question and not react with anger—a much better outcome than before.

IF YOUR CHILD IS BULLIED

If your child unfortunately becomes the victim of a bully, one of your greatest fears has been realized: Another kid has chosen to be intentionally cruel about your child's difference. And unless family and friends have been through it personally, they don't truly understand the magnitude of this punch to your gut. When your child is bullied, it feels like all your hard work in helping them live up to their greatest physical and emotional potential pales in comparison to this new challenge. Understandably, your primary instinct is to figure out the best way to help your child "bounce back" from the harsh experience. But as a parent of a child who was bullied for being different, I quickly realized there was no turning back. Rather, my role was to help him bounce forward to a new dimension of maturity and understanding.

On the morning Ethan was first bullied at school, he and our neighbor's son Javier, one of his best buddies, were playing basketball on the playground. In the middle of the game, Javi left to go to the bathroom, so Ethan began to shoot baskets on his own. Within moments, a group of fourth-grade boys approached him, pointing and scornfully snickering to one another. Immediately, Ethan nervously shoved his hands in his pockets and began looking around for Javi, praying he had returned. One of the older boys was the instigator and started audibly taunting him.

"Hey. What happened to your hands? Show them to us!"

Fearful, Ethan attempted using his go-to line. "I was born this way."

The kid wasn't satisfied. "Your hands are disgusting! Your finger looks like Captain Hook's hand!"

The other boys laughed, and Ethan began to back up until he was trapped against a tree, while the group of boys surrounded him.

The ringleader snickered, "Your fingers look like white carrots. I bet you can't do anything."

Enjoying the laughter and attention of the other boys, he continued, "No hands! No hands! You've got no hands!"

Ethan began to cry, shoving his small hands into the pockets of his shorts.

"Please let me go back," he pleaded.

But the group continued to crowd Ethan against the tree, and the head troublemaker even pushed him and cruelly added,

"Why do you need to go back? You can't do anything in school with no hands anyway." He began to laugh hysterically, and the rest joined in.

On his way back, Javier noticed what was happening to Ethan and promptly grabbed a teacher's aide to help. When they arrived, all the boys immediately dispersed.

"Ethan, are you okay?" the aide asked.

Ethan shrugged. Note to anyone: A victim of a bullying incident is never immediately okay, at least not emotionally. Don't bother asking that. Ethan was brought to the principal's office, which prompted a phone call to me. The principal couldn't reveal the names of any of the kids involved but informed me they were being reprimanded.

"Mrs. Zucker, this will never happen again. I assure you."

That evening, we were all shaken, and Ethan didn't want to go back to school. If ever he needed us, this was the moment. I knew I had to channel both my father's and my husband's dispositions and remain calm. And although it was important to let Ethan have time to cry and to validate his frustration and fears, I didn't let his pity party go on too long—there is never an upside to that. I let Ethan watch an episode of his favorite show—a big deal on a school night in our house—and we read a short book together. As much as I wanted to jump right into the day's events, it was clear he needed to unwind first.

Once we had hit enough of a pause that Ethan seemed his happy-go-lucky self, I knew it was finally my chance to help him cope. But I had to up my ante should history repeat itself. Just like Mr. Miyagi did for Daniel LaRusso in *The Karate Kid*, it was my role to prepare Ethan behind the scenes for anything to come. He would realize that although he couldn't prevent such an awful experience from happening, he could still take charge of his own reactions and understanding of events. Drawing from my coping toolbox, I again employed role-playing.

"Let's go back to that moment at recess. You play you, and I'll play the bully."

Ethan jumped in to describe the torturous experience, and how if Javier hadn't intervened with the teacher's aide, he wasn't certain what the boys would have done to him next.

I began to taunt him as he backed up to his bed. He looked anxious, so I stopped and changed gears, not wanting the experience to backfire.

"Okay! Now let's switch. You play the bully, and I will play you."

At first, I acted frightened and ashamed, purposefully hiding my hands. But then I told Ethan I was going to try something different.

"Your hands are like white carrots!" he yelled at me. I looked at him, and I stood up proudly, with my hands showing.

"I don't care what you think about me!"

This was my kid-friendly version of "What you think of me is none of my business."

Taken aback, Ethan tried again. "No hands! You've got no hands!"

Although he kept trying to bother me, I continued to appear unfazed by the attempts.

He said, "Mommy, I'm getting tired of trying to bother you."

I swelled with victory. "Exactly!"

By getting in the shoes of the bully, Ethan realized he had the power to taunt but couldn't actually control how I'd respond. As we went through the role-playing exercise together, he learned necessary skills that empowered him to face potential bullying in the future. But then Ethan asked me a question that showed me that my work wasn't complete.

"How can he hate me if he doesn't even know me?"

It became crystal clear that beyond arming him with behavioral tactics, we needed to explore what was driving the bully's viciousness in the first place.

"Consider this, E. What if his brother is really mean, and his parents ignore him? Maybe they focus on his brother because he's such a good athlete, so he's miserable."

"How do you know that, Mom?"

I reached over and put my arm around him. "I'm not sure what was really bothering any of those boys, but something is going on that has nothing to do with you. The bully lashed out at you because misery loves company."

Noting his confused expression, I explained, "That means people who are unhappy try to make others unhappy, too."

I then took it further. I drew a stick figure and then took out a kid-friendly microscope. As we examined the figure through the microscope as though it were an insect, I explained that the figure was the bully. We called him "the bully-bug," and while Ethan looked through the lens, I explained:

○ The bully-bug doesn't truly know him. To know Ethan is to love him. But—it's also true that we don't know the bully and the real reason they are choosing to be mean.

- The bully-bug doesn't actually hate him. Following up on the prior point, it is impossible to truly hate someone you don't know.

- The bully-bug is miserable. There is something else driving their behavior. "Happy kids are never mean." This is one of my favorite slogans that Ethan and I developed after he was bullied. Therefore, a kid who is cruel is attempting to shift their own sadness and insecurities to someone they believe is vulnerable to relieve their own pain.

- The bully-bug isn't truly strong. Only strong people have the ability to be kind and accepting. Weak people lash out.

- The bully-bug deserves to be pitied. Children who are different spend their lives having strangers pity them at first sight. But in fact, the bully's behavior is a major indicator of insecurity and is likely a cry for help and attention. Giving your child the ability to flip the script and pity rather than fear the bully becomes a powerful emotional weapon in managing future encounters.

Afterward, I purposefully described all of Ethan's positive qualities and added the most important point:

- People who really know you think you are awesome. Kids who know you enjoy your company. Those are the only ones who matter.

By helping Ethan decompress, step outside of the conflict, and come to the realization that the bully's behavior had much more to do with his own baggage than with Ethan, our son gained valuable perspective and was more fully prepared should history repeat itself.

LESSONS IN PERSPECTIVE

When a child who is different has been taunted, it is so easy to feel that everyone else's life is easy and not vulnerable to the same risk. I found it helped for Ethan to understand that other kids, even those who look perfect, can be the victims of bullies, too. This reminded me of a story Tracie Beer told me about her daughter, Madison. One Saturday when Madison was a kid, she went to a birthday party at a bowling alley. While waiting for her turn to bowl, she noticed that some of the other kids were making fun of a girl at the party. One of the bullies poured a bucket of popcorn over the victim's head. Immediately, several kids took her cue and started to point and laugh as the girl cried from humiliation. Feeling like she needed to do something, Madison walked over and put another bucket of popcorn over her own head in an act of support. When I asked Tracie why the girl was being bullied, her words resonated.

"Her demeanor was not the same as the rest of the girls. I guess they decided she was different."

Years later, Madison is now a high-profile singer and model who was discovered by Justin Bieber. Despite being beautiful and talented, Madison had been bullied directly on social media early in her career—proving no one is immune.

Our kids' former babysitter, Rachel Cohen, shared her own story about being bullied in school for what felt like no reason at all. It helped my kids immeasurably when she shared it with them:

I repeatedly fell victim to bullying by girls in my class. Looking back on it, I am not sure why they decided to pick on me. They just decided I was a vulnerable target and figured they could get away with it. It is surprisingly hard to decipher which incidents hurt me the most. One reason I was so hurt by the pernicious comments, texts, messages, whispers, and sneers was because they came from girls who had been nice to me in the past—girls who I thought were my friends. But they were not, even if some days they seemed "not so mean." I continually made excuses for them and for why I tried so desperately to be their friend. As a result, each day I was pounded with instant messages from unknown screen names that made fun of me and the way I looked, such as "You're ugly and have caterpillar eyebrows," "You have no friends," "You're dumb," and "Everyone hates you and your ugly curly hair." If I responded to these messages, they became more vicious. During school, the bullying continued. For instance, several girls put spitballs in my hair during class and giggled until I noticed the collection of white, crumpled scraps, which often didn't happen for hours. They made me feel stupid by ganging up on anything I said—that is, if they acknowledged my presence. At a sleepaway camp that summer, when I was twelve, some of those same girls teamed up with others and stole my food. They put an unknown substance in my shampoo and laughed about it. At one point, they twisted my picky eating habits into an eating disorder and had the entire cafeteria laughing and chanting vigorously while pounding their hands on the tables, saying, "Anorexic! Anorexic! Anorexic!" I did not have an eating disorder, but I ran out crying from humiliation.

I was so afraid to be alone that I kept trying to change myself to get them to like me again. I was lucky enough to have a supportive family who always told me not to let their mean words and looks bother me. My parents told me not to show the bullies that they hurt me because that was what they were looking for: a reason to feel powerful. In some cases, it was because they were being bullied themselves, and in others, it was for no reason at all.

A quick Internet search can produce a long list of seemingly "perfect" celebrities, athletes, and influencers who were also bullied. I found it useful to explain to my kids that difference is in the eye of the beholder. For example, Rihanna was bullied when she was a child for having light skin and green eyes, Justin Timberlake for his hair, Lady Gaga for the way she dressed, Tom Cruise because he struggled with reading, Shaquille O'Neal for his size and for having a stutter as a child. Taylor Swift says that being bullied actually gave her the inspiration to write her songs. Even Kate Middleton, Princess of Wales, was mercilessly bullied at school for no apparent reason at all. There are tons of other examples your child will be even more familiar with that you can choose from. Most important, each of these influential figures learned how to overcome mockery about something they couldn't control, rather than let the experience thwart future success.

MOTIVATING THE BYSTANDER

There is a term called "Ubuntu," which means "I am who I am because of who we all are." Archbishop Desmond Tutu, the South African human rights leader, described it best: In embracing the concept of Ubuntu, we "believe that a person is a person through other persons. That my humanity is caught up, bound up, inextricably, with yours. When I dehumanize you, I dehumanize myself. The solitary human being is a contradiction in terms. Therefore you seek to work for the common good because your humanity comes into its own in community, in belonging."

In raising our sons, I've longed for them to grow up in the warm embrace of an Ubuntu culture. But kids must be taught to relate to one another not despite but even because of their differences. I've observed that many elementary and middle schools have tried to prevent or stop bullying by hanging posters in hallways and classrooms that encourage students to "Choose Kindness." Although the message is certainly an important goal, it reminds me of the half-baked "Just Say No" campaigns in the late 1980s that were part of the U.S. War on Drugs. Does a sign on a wall actually influence behavior? Certainly, parents should urge their kids to be pleasant and respectful to other kids. That is easily said *and* done. After all, it takes only a split second to say hello to a kid who is different in the hallway. But choosing kindness alone is not enough. I've always felt that the campaigns should be titled "Choose Friendship," accompanied by efforts to teach empathy and acceptance.

After Ethan was bullied, I piloted a social and emotional learning program in Ethan's elementary school to help promote empathy among the students. I was convinced that the kids who taunted our son had never considered what it felt like to experience life through his eyes, judged and misunderstood. The pilot ultimately became a successful national program called Kids Flaunt that was offered in collaboration with Scholastic Inc., to all U.S. public and private elementary schools.

The first day I visited Ethan's class to introduce Kids Flaunt, I was exuberant. I'd developed a theme, "The things that make me different make me, me," and prompted students to share their own visible or invisible differences, which was meant to help them better relate and even empathize with our son. But instead, several kids approached me.

"Excuse me, Mrs. Zucker. I am not different," one stated confidently, immediately followed by others, all proudly concluding the same.

Their reactions disappointed me but were extremely informative. Certain kids are willing to taunt others, especially those they can't identify with. In order for my kids to feel accepted by their peers and vice versa, it was essential that these other kids see themselves as different, too. They needed to accept that, in fact, everyone is different in their own way.

It was time for me to think outside the box. I turned to one of the boys who I knew was on the playground the day of the incident.

"Isn't your mom from Spain? How would you feel if someone made fun of her accent?" The boy nodded, walked back to his desk, and began to scribble on his paper.

Later that evening, I received a call from the parent of another child in the class. Her daughter had epilepsy, something she'd been hiding until she participated in Kids Flaunt. Suddenly, she was provided a platform to share that she'd had nearly five hundred seizures per day and had been in the hospital numerous times because of it.

"Meg, I don't know how to thank you. She's already asked the teacher if she could not only read her essay aloud, but also give a presentation about her condition and include pictures of herself taken at the hospital."

Apparently, the project struck a chord. For that girl, having her peers confess and describe their own visible and invisible differences, and then empathize with each other, catapulted her from a place of shame about her condition to a desire to, well . . . flaunt.

By the time Ethan was in fourth grade, he'd been featured in a Scholastic *Storyworks* magazine article written by best-selling author Lauren Tarshis, titled "The Awesome Powers of Ethan Z." In the article, Ethan advised, "If a person can't accept you, then they are not a friend. And if that person isn't a friend, then you shouldn't care about what that person thinks of you."

He had certainly come a long way since he'd been bullied

on the playground in first grade. In response to the piece, Ethan received many letters from grade school students across the country. I was particularly startled by their willingness to share their own version of being different, wanting Ethan to know that they could directly relate and were inspired by his story. Here are several examples from the letters Ethan received:

- *"I really liked your story and I am also different because when I am bullied I do not stand up for myself . . . In my class there is someone who hates my guts and calls me stupid. Next time she bothers me I would like to try your method . . ."*

- *"I am different too because I am very sensitive to other people's feelings and even cry when they cry. When people are rude to me, I am going to try not caring what other people think of me. Since it worked for you, I am sure it will work for me . . ."*

- *"I will tell my friends about your method. There is a big bully in our school and we think it will work. Thanks for helping me . . ."*

- *"I enjoyed reading about you in class. It is amazing the way you act. I hope you understand how great you really are. I am different because people teased me when I was new at camp. I cried. I will now try to be like you and say, 'I don't care what you think about me!' You taught me to be the bigger person."*

- *"About one week ago someone was hitting, kicking, and tackling me, and then threw a football hard in my face. The person said I messed up the game. Later that day we read your* Storyworks *article and I remembered what you said, and later that day I said, 'I don't care what you think about me' to the kid and walked away . . ."*

- *"I am different because I am scared of all fish—even the dead ones! Even though nobody knows, it is nothing to tease me about and that should be the same with you . . ."*

- *"I am different because three people in my family have celiac and two have autism. As for me, I have a HUGE birthmark on my lip. I like how you can just say, 'I don't care what you think about me,' and mean it. . . . I'll always remember to practice like you did with your mom so I'll have awesome powers just like you . . ."*

- *"I am different because I like different books and music than my friends. . . . I will try your method when the bullies bother me . . ."*

- *"I am different because I don't care much about rock stars or looking good or being in fashion. At camp I hung up an Angry Birds poster instead of a Bieber poster and was teased. I will try your method next summer . . ."*

- *"I am different because my arms are very hairy. I have never seen someone like you, it's really special. You can do anything, and you make me feel like everyone is different, not just me. I think you are the coolest person I have ever seen . . ."*

- *"I am different because I have curly, poofy hair and I have celiac disease. Last year someone called me unlucky and made me sad. I cannot wait to use your methods when people bother me about my food."*

- *"I am different because I am very tall for my age. Some people call me names or try to climb on me. I did what you said and they went away!"*

Most kids thankfully do not wish to hurt another kid on an emotional level, but that doesn't mean they're willing to help someone else who is being bullied. Along with supporting our own child, it's just as critical to encourage our kids' teachers to help students recognize and even take pride in their own unique qualities. Once kids realize they wouldn't want to be mocked or taunted because of something *they* cannot change about themselves, they're more likely to not only empathize with victims, but also to help them.

THE UPSIDE

I've learned that kids who have been bullied can emerge not only stronger and wiser, but also eager to help others get through it, too. One example comes from ten-year-old Peyton Chandler, another past winner of our Kids Flaunt contest:

Because of my cleft palate, people have bullied me. One called me "upper-lip kid." This brought me anxiety, and when I was younger, every night I would cry myself to sleep. I used to punch holes in the wall to deal with anger, so I have taken anger management classes. In third grade, I had massive meltdowns every day because of my brother's friends and other people. There was a friend that helped me through all of my issues. He said, "I was teased for having a cleft palate too, and I just walked away. Look at me now, I am working at McDonald's for $15.00 an hour!"

In my life, I have had ten surgeries beginning at five months old, and my last one was this past summer. I don't like the way they say to me, "Say goodbye to your parents" before surgery. It seemed to me it meant I wouldn't see them again. I still need to have more surgeries and I'm afraid. When I have surgery, I need special medicine to fall asleep and it makes me act really strangely and differently. It's not an easy process.

In the future, I will help other people that go through what I have been through. When I am seventeen, my surgeries will be done, and I'd like to tell others about cleft palates and how to handle the stress. It's hard to handle a cleft palate with all the teasing, and people being mean and rude, but I'm glad I have a cleft palate. You're probably, like, why exactly? Because I have had the experience.

Donna Agostino empowered her daughter Victoria through her own experience of being bullied in fourth grade. When Victoria was initially diagnosed with alopecia, which is an autoimmune disorder that causes massive hair loss, she was feeling apprehensive. At that point, Donna wasn't sure to what extent Victoria's hair might continue to fall out and had shared what was happening with only a few friends. To her dismay, one day in class, a clump of hair fell onto Victoria's desk. Distressed, she couldn't move and just stared at it, not knowing what to do. A few moments passed before the teacher helped scoop the wad of her locks into a plastic bag for Victoria to bring home. A few kids began to whisper, but the teacher pressed on with her lesson plan. Victoria was relieved until later in the cafeteria, when a girl named Betsy, who was in Victoria's class, approached her in a mocking tone.

"Oh, I heard you got a haircut!"

Victoria already knew that Betsy had a reputation for being mean, and Victoria had even confided to Donna the summer before school began that she hoped she wouldn't be in Betsy's class. Trying to defuse the situation, Victoria began describing her condition. Because it was close to the holidays (and not because she was intentionally trying to hide her bald spots), Victoria was wearing a Santa hat at lunch. She tugged nervously at it.

Betsy detected her uneasiness and yelled for everyone to hear, "Ewwww! That's disgusting! Don't go near Victoria. . . . She has lice!"

Humiliated, Victoria began to cry. And still wanting to prove to the other kids that she didn't have lice, Victoria thrust off her hat. The damage was done, however. Everyone was staring at her while Betsy sneered in satisfaction.

Back at home, Donna hugged her daughter and was grateful

they were close enough that Victoria confided everything to her. Donna knew that the incident was beyond a typical outburst from a curious kid. It was her job to not only console her daughter but help her move past the experience.

"Have you ever thought about the fact that Betsy's actions are about who she is and not really about you?"

Victoria looked up.

"What if we put her in a bully category?"

"Mom, I already know she's a bully . . ."

"What I mean is that if we decide that someone is in the 'Bully Bucket,' then we know once we've placed them there that we don't ever have to internalize anything they say about us."

Knowing she had Victoria's attention, Donna continued: "She makes you feel bad to make herself feel better. If anyone is ever intentionally mean like that, just decide whether they are in the Bully Bucket or not. It's like having a power—if we place them in the Bully Bucket, then we know what to expect from them and we just don't care."

Fortunately, because the principal intervened the next day, Betsy didn't bother Victoria again at school. But as a result of that single experience, Donna learned that Victoria had developed the inner strength to move forward. One day Victoria asked if she could have something printed on the back of a sweatshirt.

Donna responded, "Sure, what do you have in mind?"

"Mom, I want to have a bull on it with the words 'Don't mess with me. I'm a Taurus!'"

It was at that moment that Donna knew helping her daughter get through the bullying experience had actually made Victoria stronger. When Donna recalled the story to me, she added, "Ya know, Meg. It is no wonder Victoria's favorite motto is: 'Even with one wing you can fly.'"

And there is one final upside worth noting. When a child is bullied simply because other kids decided they are different, the experience causes them to approach life going forward with a newfound sense of empathy. A girl named Cassidy Weitzer underscores the point with her own story of being bullied as a child:

I may not look different, but it doesn't mean I haven't felt judged. When I was eight years old, I was picked on by a group of popular girls. They decided I was different from them, so they didn't get to know me. It really affected me, and I didn't want to go to school because of them. It was really hard, but it taught me not to judge someone without getting to know them. I also learned how important it was to share what I was feeling with my parents.

In my school, kids can be really mean to others without knowing them. I wish that everyone could be treated equally without being judged based on their looks, personality, or background. One time there was a kid who was in a class of kids that needed extra help, and he would come for a class on computers. Just because he was in that class, people wouldn't like him and they would laugh at him, and he would get really angry. Just because they didn't give him a chance, they could have missed out on a great friend. Certain kids think it's cool to make fun of other kids to fit in with the popular kids, but it's not.

I think kids can treat other people badly because they have their own insecurities. I also think my experience being judged by other kids taught me a lot about how to treat other kids, and that it's really cool to give everyone a chance. Just put yourself in their shoes! Based on my experience, whatever difference you may have, it is important to stand up for yourself or another kid that is being judged or even bullied for being different. It could change their life. It changed mine.

No one wishes a bully's torture on their worst enemy. According to the *Cambridge Dictionary*, taking the bull by the horns means "to do something difficult in a brave and determined way." A kid is fortunate when they have parents and other family members who help them face their fears and discover they are more resilient than they ever realized. Therefore, being stuck in a never-ending loop of torment doesn't have to be the final chapter of their story. Instead, you have the ability to show them the road map to rise above and beyond the bullying. And ironically, if your child is bullied because they are different, the very thing that triggered the taunts is also the reason they can be stronger than most to manage it. With you in their corner, your child has an even stronger sense of self, and they're no longer as vulnerable.

CONCLUSION

What used to be my biggest fear—having a child who is different—turned out to be my greatest gift. But first, let me keep it real. When something doesn't go according to plan, anyone's first inclination is to fix the issue. When you learn your child is different, however, it is like crash-landing into an unstoppable new reality. You are overwhelmed with feelings of insecurity and uncertainty. What felt like years of being in control are behind you, and the new road feels frightening and the unknown terrifying. Your close friends and family can no longer fully relate, and their ability to support you in just the way you need is not guaranteed. In the meantime, your mind is consumed with anxiety and understandable questions:

- Will I have the necessary strength for my child to be able to emotionally depend on me?

- Will I be able to help them function independently?

- Will they be able to not only cope but even blossom without me?

- Will they lead a "normal" life?

- Will they be accepted by their peers?

- Will they blame me?

- Will I ever stop feeling guilty?

There truly isn't time to take a breather and adjust, but somehow you discover an inner strength you didn't even know existed. At first, success is measured by the extent to which your child can become capable within their means. As I've followed my own parents' "let go and let live" philosophy, I've felt immensely thankful to witness my children's accomplishments, which have exceeded even my own expectations. And it is undeniable that the more I resisted the urge to overprotect, the more they blossomed. The inverse is also true—the more I unnecessarily intervened, the more I stifled their progress and the more they even regressed.

But because kids who are different must live life in what feels like a fishbowl, success also means helping them internalize a most important concept: You are not what the world thinks of you. You are what *you* think of you.

"Flaunting" is code for unconditional self-acceptance. It is your mission, therefore, to embrace it and help your child live to their fullest potential. But sure, it's not fun being the subject of constant curiosity, endless outbursts of pity, or in the worst scenario, cruelty. So your child is certainly entitled to have their down days. But you become their unmovable rock, their biggest advocate. With you and the rest of the family in their corner, your child will come to understand that feeling sorry for themselves is exhausting. They'll lean on you, and you'll delight in their progress and growth. Together, you'll cherish the discovery that letting go of worry about what others think is both powerful and freeing. One day it will hit you—it is time to rejoice because of both your own and your child's immense inner strength.

There are also notable perks of being different. Imagine effectively living your life in a bubble of love where the only people who want to know and befriend you are caring, kind, and not superficial. This will be their life's blessing. And because of this, they won't sweat the small stuff. Simply put, life can be difficult for anyone, but when your child is supported in the way they need, they become the sturdiest version of themselves. They and their siblings also accept others without judgment and with authentic empathy. In short, they bring beauty into your lives and the world just by being themselves. Having a child who is different is a gift that keeps on giving. The more they demonstrate being fully comfortable in their own skin, the more magnetic they become; others will be encouraged to follow their lead and to fully embrace their own visible or invisible differences.

But something has always gnawed at me. If my parents were so brilliant in their own method of raising me, a child born with such a blatant difference, why did I hide my hands in shame in public, while our sons have not repeated that behavior? Sure, they have me as their role model now, but I'm convinced there's more to it than that. Recently, initiatives to promote acceptance have expanded beyond diversity, equity, and inclusion to encompass another important concept: *Belonging*. Thankfully, due to technological advancements and safe social media groups and communities, people are more connected than ever, no matter where they reside. So these days, children who are different are afforded an opportunity that I didn't have in my youth—to know they are not alone.

One common thread expressed to me by so many parents who have raised children who are different is worth sharing: In hindsight, we wouldn't trade it for anything. Truly. I believe that is because we have come to appreciate that the most meaningful parts of our lives are the ones we once feared the most but then overcame. My husband, John, and I often joke that our family's best-kept secret is that people who encounter us immediately jump to the conclusion that our lives must be a long winding road on the struggle-bus. That couldn't be further from the truth. My own deepest feelings of gratitude have come from knowing our kids are admirable and thriving not *despite* but rather *because* they are different. Difference has become something they not only accept about themselves but that we all choose to celebrate. You will, too.

ADDITIONAL WORDS OF WISDOM

One of the benefits of running my nonprofit organization, Don't Hide It, Flaunt It, has been the opportunity to hear from countless other parents of children who are different. They all have their own nuggets of wisdom to share. While not everyone's experience and path is identical, and challenges and setbacks are inevitable, unforeseen fulfillment, key insights, and unexpected joy prevail. We can all learn something valuable from these collective admissions, regrets, revelations, and expressions of candor, gratitude, hope, and promise. These are some of my favorites.

—Meg

LIVE IN THE MOMENT
by Mitzi Schuller

My daughter Pam is a successful, educated, hilarious young woman who lives in New York City and makes a living as a comedian, speaker, and disability advocate. If you had asked when she was in high school if any of this would be possible, everyone who knew her, including me, would have replied with a resounding *"No."*

Pam has Tourette's syndrome, a neurological disorder that means she has involuntary "tics" that cause her to shrug her shoulders, blink her eyes, and unexpectedly blurt out noises. When Pam was an adolescent, she had such a serious case of Tourette's that the doctors told me they had never seen such a severe case. In fact, Pam's condition was so acute that she couldn't attend school in person for years and had broken bones, including in her neck, from her uncontrollable physical moments. My heart broke as she became socially isolated.

Reflecting on raising Pam, I wish I had lived more in the moment. I spent so many sleepless nights worrying about how Pam was going to make it on her own. How would she take care of herself? How could she independently exist in this world? I missed the opportunity to enjoy what she brought to our lives because I was so terrified for her future. It didn't help that a lot of people assumed the worst, often warning me to lower my expectations. For example, one middle school teacher insisted that Pam would never get into college because she had Tourette's. I wish I had put less weight on the incessantly negative opinions and instead absorbed more of the positive. From the beginning of her life, Pam deserved for me to discover and celebrate who she was and to find joy in her disability—to be her guiding light and let her know that everything would be fine. Instead, due to her own strong spirit and determination (and wicked sense of humor), Pam led *me* down that path. I wasted a lot of years trying to make things better for Pam. Instead, I should have worked harder to find the personal strength to embrace and accept everything beautiful she embodied.

GRIEF IS AN IMPORTANT PROCESS
by Jamie Chandler

I have the privilege of being Peyton's mom. Peyton was born with a cleft lip and palate. The day Peyton arrived was filled with excitement. He was born by a planned C-section, and his father and I could not wait to meet him. Doctors were ready and everything was going as planned . . . until the entire room went still. At that moment I knew something was not "right." When the team held Peyton up so we could see him, I realized right away Peyton was special.

After days in the NICU and recovery, we came home and were able to settle into our regular life. But internally, something didn't feel right. As a mom, I knew I should be feeling happy and excited to have added a new miracle to our household. I found myself almost grieving for something I felt was missing, however.

Although I was ashamed of how I felt, I shared my feelings with family, close friends, and my doctors. I opened my heart and found that through my grief, Peyton was exactly where he needed to be, and we needed him. Throughout his life, Peyton has taught us about true strength, advocacy, and overcoming life's challenges. He has an unexpected maturity that can't be explained. As a toddler, Peyton sought out others who seemed lonely. He would walk up to strangers in the park and begin talking to them. Even at a young age, he seemed to understand the importance of inclusion. Our life is truly blessed, thanks to Peyton. He is the last piece to our puzzle. Grief has been an important process for me. It helped me to accept the losses of "what might have been" and appreciate the blessings I have now.

REFUSING COMPARISON
by Betsy Drew

I am Betsy Drew. My daughter Kendra Gottsleben is an author, advocate, spokesperson, model, friend, and marketing communications specialist, and has a rare disease called mucopolysaccharidosis type VI (MPS Type VI). One in 215,000 people are diagnosed with this condition. In essence, Kendra's body is missing the enzyme needed to cleanse her cells, which results in a buildup of a gluey-like substance that affects her heart, eyes, connective tissue, and other vital organs.

Overall, Kendra's disability wasn't a constant focus when she was growing up. While we didn't ignore it, I simply saw my daughter as capable of achieving what she wanted to achieve. As her mother, I was committed to helping Kendra focus on her greatest strengths, gifts, and talents, never succumbing to self-pity or defaulting to the word "can't" in her vocabulary. But even though my message to Kendra was to always push forward, sometimes I silently wondered whether I was pushing her too much. I never wanted to be the one to limit what she chose to accomplish. Also, I discovered that focusing on the future caused me many sleepless nights in fear. Mostly, I worried about the difficulties Kendra might have to face.

But what helped the most was refusing to compare Kendra to her peers. Instead, we concentrated on what might be possible. Being truthful to my daughter was a priority for me. When Kendra asked questions about her small stature, difficulty walking, and strangers' stares, I told her that we all have differences, but hers are more visible than others'. Most important, it was my duty to help Kendra understand that the world was not always going to acknowledge her frustrations. It was up to her to gain a positive outlook on life, and her determination and perseverance would not only help her personally but would make an even larger imprint on the world.

When I was an elementary school administrator and teacher, I leveraged my own personal experience raising Kendra and discovered that my insights could also help others. Because of my profession, I was afforded the opportunity to advise many parents of children with disabilities. In that context, I encouraged parents to look down the road, but not too far. Now an adult, Kendra has proven that my worries were a waste. She has proven to me through her success in life that, beyond her own achievements, you never know the impact your child can also have on other people's lives.

SPEAK OPENLY TO YOUR CHILD
by Monique Herrera

My name is Monique, and I am a wife and mother of two amazing boys. Matthew, my eldest, was born with a visual impairment (bilateral optic nerve coloboma, strabismus, and nystagmus). Matthew does not have vision in his right eye and has low vision in his left eye (20/200). He uses large print but also knows how to read and write braille. Likely the greatest coincidence of my life is that before getting pregnant with Matthew, I had been working at a school for the blind for four years.

There are no simple answers when parenting a child with a disability. We started by accepting Matthew's diagnosis. My husband and I speak candidly about it and are happy to educate others. When Matthew turned three, we began explaining to him that he had a visual impairment. Speaking openly gave Matthew the confidence to ask questions about his condition, voice his frustrations, and advocate for himself.

Throughout elementary school, we asked Matthew's teacher for the blind (teacher for the visually impaired, or TVI) to do presentations for his classroom peers and school staff. The TVI had Matthew present the information to his peers as he grew older. At every presentation, he made braille labels with each student's name and demonstrated the tools he was using in class. Matthew felt special, as he had this "special secret code" (braille) that he could teach other students. I am hopeful that the other kids shared what Matthew taught with their parents, siblings, and other neighborhood kids so that when they encounter Matthew in our community, they will be educated. Knowledge is what breaks barriers.

As his parents, we want Matthew to be confident and proud so he has the runway to a bright future. It is our goal for Matthew to grow up self-reliant, while accepting that adaptations or help can lead to his own independence. Most important, we work to ensure that Matthew understands that the tools he may need to help him see are not a measurement of him as a person and his ability to thrive.

I hope and pray that the people he meets accept him for who he is and not his limitations, the same way we all want to be seen and treated.

LEARNING TO USE MY VOICE
by Stacey Monsen

My daughter E had been in speech therapy at our local children's hospital for about six months when I finally asked the question I hadn't been able to say aloud.

"Why are we here, and are you concerned about my daughter E's development?"

The speech therapist suggested that we speak with our pediatrician. When I braced myself and took that next step, I learned that she was concerned. E had developmental delays and repetitive behaviors that suggested she was on the autism spectrum. The doctor gave me a list of developmental pediatricians to call and get a formal evaluation.

"I know this sucks," she said. This life-altering conversation happened over the phone, and she did not call back to check on us the next day, or week, or even month.

After a three-month wait, when she was two and a half, E was diagnosed with autism. I felt simultaneously relieved and scared. Looking back, I could see that there were signs. I had never really interacted with anyone, adult or child, on the spectrum, however, so I just did not know what signs to look for. No one could really tell us what to expect for the future with E.

Having both come from dysfunctional families, my husband

and I hoped to create a family together that we hadn't personally experienced. He even wanted to stay home and raise our children. As many parents do, we had an idealized vision of the life we wanted to lead, which suddenly looked different than our reality.

I took some time off from work to make therapy appointments, apply for day treatment, and just process my new normal. My boss at the time was traveling for work so I sent an e-mail informing her of the diagnosis and that I would be taking some time off. When I returned to work, she met with me in person to check in to see how I was doing. Toward the end of our conversation, whether intentional or not, she said something extremely hurtful.

"You don't need to tell people about your problems."

I was so stunned, I was at a loss for words. In that moment I felt devastatingly alone. The realization came crashing in like a hard, cold wave. What my family was going through and who my child was—these were things to be ashamed of.

A few weeks later, I was sitting at a team lunch and one of the senior leaders was going around and asking everyone about their children and families. People began to describe their summer activities, potty training, age-appropriate milestones, and so on. When it was my turn to be asked, I was skipped over. Admittedly, it was both a relief and a curse since I felt extremely anxious not knowing what I was going to say. I became two Staceys: Work Stacey and Home Stacey.

At home I was a mother trying to figure out my new normal with therapies, day treatments, communication tools, and a lack of sleep—just trying to keep it all together. I did not fit in with my "mom" friends anymore. In book club, moms would talk about wanting to get their kids to eat cold squash soup, while I simply wanted my daughter to talk, to say the word "Mom." At work, I continued to project this image of perfection. Over time I mastered the skill of deflecting questions about my daughter. If someone asked me how my daughter was doing or what milestone she was hitting, I would reply with a very generic "She's great, thanks for asking!" My go-to trick to deflect was to immediately ask how their child was or change the subject entirely. Only a trusted few knew both Staceys.

About six years ago, I came very close to having a breakdown. E needed 24/7 care due to self-harm, and I was totally sleep-deprived and had only a single-family income and little savings because of medical bills. Extended family tensions and working in a very high-stress, fast-paced environment where perfection was valued made everything that much harder.

I slowly began to merge the two Staceys and to share my story. Over the years, I have learned that I have unique insights and skill sets because of my experience. I am using my voice as an advocate/ally to break down the stigma around disability in both personal and professional contexts.

Now as a leader in my profession, I have made certain that the behaviors I had personally experienced at work are not repeated. I will always ask someone about their child, family, or themselves with genuine care and make them feel supported and included in every conversation, however they wish to contribute.

LIFE IS NOT HARDER, IT'S DEEPER
by Liz Svatek

Fifty-two days. That's how long we spent in the hospital after my son Landon's birth. I had to have an emergency C-section, and the trauma led him to have a stroke. Landon was born with right arterial thrombosis, which is a fancy way of saying he was born with blood clots in his right arm. This has led to tons of scarring and limited mobility. He was in jeopardy of having his arm amputated and he almost died. They called it a "lightning strike" event, and it was. All I knew is that I was unconditionally committed to my son. There will never be another Landon Svatek. When he was born with a physical difference, I couldn't help but feel that my dreams for his future, in many respects, had died. My mind kept focusing on the fact that he would not have the life I'd imagined for him. His life would be harder. I even found myself angry with God. Why was this Landon's cross to bear?

I will never forget Landon's first day of preschool. Not because I was scared to leave him like all the other moms were scared to leave their children, but because I was terrified that he would *need* me. How would he be able to open a door, communicate what happened to his arm, fend off any unwanted comments? I learned that despite my fears, Landon had a strength I hadn't considered. He has had to walk into situations where I surely would have fallen apart and given up. Despite having endured over forty surgeries, constant physical therapy, and stares from strangers—Landon is happy. He has the kind of joy that's like a lightbulb inside of him. No matter what happens, he takes it all in stride like it's a normal day in his life. And it is.

Landon has never blamed God. In fact, it's quite the opposite. One morning after attending a teen church group, he told me they discussed blaming God for things that happen to them. I asked him if he mentioned his arm. He looked at me kind of quizzically and then said, "My arm is not a good example of that." Then he continued, "My arm is how I connect with God and how He connects with me." Tears sprang to my eyes. This arm, this source of suffering and constant management in his life, was his connection to God. After I composed myself, I told him that some adults never achieve this level of spirituality and faith. He told me, "I could never blame God, He's my friend."

Landon is now fourteen, and I have realized that his life is not a harder life, but rather, it's a deeper life. Because he was born with his difference, his life is filled with purpose and meaning. A life I couldn't have imagined for him those days I wept in fear for his future, but one that I now stand in awe of. Many parents will tell me that when their kids are experiencing a difficult time, they will remark, "Think of Landon, look how strong he is, look at what he's been through." I'm glad Landon is a source of strength and a shining light helping others to approach their own circumstances with strength and positivity. I couldn't have predicted it at his birth, but there is no question that by having Landon, our lives have forever been changed for the better.

LISTEN MORE AND REACT LESS
by Melanie Aube

My son Brennan was born with ear and facial anomalies that created hearing loss and a sweet, crooked smile! He is now a healthy, active middle schooler who, like every other kid, just wants to be included and accepted by his peers. As a mom, I want to give Brennan tools to grow and thrive with confidence and grace. The funny thing is that no matter how much I read, research, or pray for the best way to do this, I really have no answers! What's taught me the most is simply being Brennan's mom.

What I mean is that I've learned to listen more and react less, breathe more and take a pause, ultimately giving him the grace he needs to experience all of the physical and emotional peaks and valleys of his journey. Listening fatigue and thoughtless and unkind treatment from peers have caused extreme physical and mental exhaustion for Brennan. He often opens the car door at the end of the school day and subsequently "unloads." In these moments, I have learned to listen and give Brennan space to express himself instead of instantly offering advice.

By no means do I always get this right, so I have learned to give myself a little bit of that grace, too. I realize that allowing Brennan the space and time to "unload" helps him to reset and move forward with purpose. Although we do our best to live "typically" and not allow a difference to define Brennan, the reality is that life isn't "typical" for him, and that is okay. At times, I think I need to fix everything for Brennan when the road gets bumpy, but that would mean stealing *his* journey!

Brennan doesn't need me to fix a thing. He is both strong and clever enough to navigate life in his own way. He just needs me to be there to champion him and to be a soft place to fall. When we allow ourselves a moment to recognize the messy, challenging parts of this adventure, we are able to move forward and clearly see the beauty, support, and acceptance it provides.

THE REALIZATION THAT I COULDN'T "FIX" THIS
by Cathy Marcus

My name is Cathy, and I like to control things. I prefer that things go according to plan—my plan, that is. I really don't like to deviate from my plan and sometimes even double down on my plan when things go awry. Which is the absolute worst strategy when your child is struggling.

My daughter Lexi has some significant learning disabilities that are turbocharged by anxiety. Or maybe the anxiety is turbocharged by the learning disabilities. We'll never know. Lexi struggled mightily through grammar school, where there was a "one size fits all" approach to teaching that did not accommodate someone with both dyslexia and processing challenges, and the onus was on the student to make that approach work. I just kept executing my plan and was stuck in the school's "one size fits all" trap, instead of pivoting to a "Lexi has learning disabilities and is struggling" plan. I kept charging through brick walls to find a solution—one more tutor, one more therapist, one more medication. If I just worked harder, read more, and found the right help, I could "fix" this. Meanwhile, the academic struggles and stress were metastasizing, attacking Lexi's self-esteem and dimming her smile that had once brimmed with dimples.

Lexi did not need fixing, and I wish it hadn't taken me so long to realize that. She needed a cheerleader, not someone blindly executing a generic plan that wasn't even working. My daughter needed me to champion the "Lexi can be happy and successful" cause from the start. I regret the years we lost and wish that I had become her champion much earlier. Lexi is now grown, having earned her master's degree in social work. Most important, my daughter is happy, successful, and very resilient—one of the lifelong benefits of her early struggles. Being Lexi's mom has taught me it is never too late to pivot to the right plan and watch your child soar.

TAKE OPPORTUNITIES TO EDUCATE OTHERS
by Jennifer Gottlieb

Hi! My name is Jen, and my husband, Adam, and I have a son named Cole who was born with spastic quadriplegia cerebral palsy. One day, when Cole was in second grade, we were walking in a store, and a friendly little girl from Cole's school came up to us to say hello. Her mother turned to her and said something in Spanish. I understood what she had said to her daughter, and I could not believe what I had heard; she said, "Get away from him; he is sick!" Although my skin is quite thick, my heart sank. All I could imagine was the little girl going back to school and telling other students to stay away from Cole because he was sick. They started to walk away, and I knew I had to think on my feet.

Together with Cole, I decided to approach the mother in a nonconfrontational way, using my best Spanish. Her little girl was still with her.

"Excuse me, my son is not sick," I explained. "He just walks differently."

The mother replied, "Oh, I didn't know."

After Cole and I left, I was grateful I had the chance to clear up her misunderstanding. I longed for them both to learn that just because Cole is different doesn't mean something is wrong with him.

A young child is very impressionable and takes cues from their parents. While that can be a wonderful thing, it can also be a hindrance if parents pass along misinformation to their kids. As Cole's biggest advocate, I find that it can be best to directly address ill-informed parents, since I have the opportunity and knowledge to educate them. This way, their child is provided the information they need when they encounter a child like Cole, and then we can all move on.

ALL WE HAD TO DO WAS FOLLOW HIS LEAD
by Rebecca Baeurle

Our son Alex was born with a rare skeletal disorder known as Holt-Oram syndrome. As a result, his arms are not full-length and are only partially functional; he also has inwardly turned hands and no thumbs. Of course, we worried about everything. . . . Would he be able to feed himself, dress himself, use the toilet on his own? Would he be able to write? Would he have friends? Would he be able to participate in activities? Ride a bike? Drive a car? The list was endless.

The first five years of his life, Alex underwent multiple corrective surgeries to position his hands for maximum functionality and to create a thumb on the hand that can reach his face, so he would have an opposable grip. All this with the goal of having him enter kindergarten with his peers. So at age five, off he went as we held our breath.

One by one, Alex dispelled each of our fears. He overcame every challenge he faced and simply did things his own way. And he didn't just conquer everyday challenges, he pursued his interests. Alex plays basketball, skis, skimboards, draws, writes music, and even plays guitar. Because Alex is very comfortable in his own skin, has a big personality, and makes friends easily, his school-age years were quite seamless. But when it was time for him to go off to college in a new community, once again we worried about whether he would be accepted. Well, that was a silly concern. Not only did Alex immediately pledge his desired fraternity, but by the second semester, he was voted to be recruitment chair.

All we have had to do was follow his lead and watch how Alex continues to fearlessly live his life. Simply put, he doesn't let his "limitations" limit him. Recently Alex said something that reminded me that all my worries were unfounded. "Mom,

I don't mind being different. People remember me." That's our Alex! I couldn't be prouder.

FINDING AN OUTLET FOR MYSELF
by Naomi Shapiro

My six-year-old, Leor, was born with 18q deletion syndrome, meaning a portion of his eighteenth chromosome is missing. This syndrome can result in a large spectrum of medical and developmental issues, including small stature, hearing loss, heart abnormalities, and intellectual or developmental disability, among other things. The level of severity varies widely—no two people have the same manifestations, and no one has all of them. When Leor was born, we were not aware that he had a chromosomal abnormality. He spent the first seven weeks of his life in the NICU due to respiratory and feeding issues. We received the news of his 18q deletion after about two weeks. I remember that the genetic counselor left us feeling pretty raw and shocked. Learning about the possibilities of what Leor's life might look like was staggering. A few days later, in a conversation with Leor's doctor, I asked her, "What are we supposed to do?" She said, "You are going to take him home and love him." Truly, I needed that directive. I was so lost in the what-ifs, the newly acquired medical jargon, and the shock, that I forgot this most important detail.

We brought Leor home and, of course, loved him. Caring for Leor as an infant at home was overwhelming, scary, and isolating. Over time, it all became easier, both because we got more comfortable and experienced, and also because he became less fragile as he grew. At every stage of his life, I have had to work hard at maintaining a sense of self. Sometimes parenthood in general can pull us to focus so much on our children that we forget about ourselves. I find that is even more true with Leor, as his medical and developmental needs are ongoing for the foreseeable future. I am proud of the mother that I am to both of my boys and the ways in which I have navigated Leor's needs. But also, finding an outlet to be myself apart from being the mom of a medically complex child has been important for my mental well-being. For me, maintaining close friendships, furthering my career, and being part of a community—my synagogue—have helped me keep an equilibrium, which in turn makes me a better parent. The things that help a parent maintain a sense of self can look different for each person.

The first few months of Leor's life required so much focus. Even in that incredibly busy, draining period, I tried to be in contact with friends, whether through a short call, a text, or a walk. I needed small reminders of who I was beyond the confines of this new world I had entered. Being part of a community that has given me support has not only been important to me, but also to Leor, his brother, and my husband. Maintaining a sense of self has not always been easy or even possible, but I continue to strive for it.

NO EXPECTATIONS, JUST EXPERIENCES
by Mark Mahaney

My son Noah has Down syndrome and autism. Although he has three brothers, Noah's my boy who most often makes me appreciate the smaller things—the most important things in life. Everything comes more slowly for Noah. But it does come. And when it comes, you really, really, really appreciate it. When at twelve, Noah walked up to the counter and verbalized "chocolate ice cream" for the first time, I appreciated it. When at fourteen, he strolled over to a friend and for the first time gave him a high-five while loudly shouting, "Hey, buddy," I appreciated it. And when at age sixteen, he started to say "thank you" before and after a request, I appreciated it. Lately Noah likes to dance extemporaneously while shouting, "DJ Khaled." And I continue to appreciate every moment like this.

People have all types of different reactions to, or experiences with, special needs children. I fully understand that having such a child can be challenging, scary, perhaps even terrifying. I have also witnessed and experienced the uncertainty and awkwardness that both children and adults exhibit when encountering special needs children. It's all very understandable.

What most people who encounter our family don't realize, however, is that my experience with Noah has been wonderful. He is both my most playful child and my wisest soul. He is a source of immense tranquility to me. No expectations. Just experiences. Noah is unconditional love to me. And for that, I am extremely grateful.

As a parent of a special needs child, I sometimes get asked if there is anything friends can do to help. There isn't really. At least, there's nothing special you need to do. Just be yourself.

I BECAME THAT MOM
by Debbie Kass

My name is Debbie, and my child's name is Chloe. At age five, Chloe became sick with a virus that left her paralyzed and unable to breathe on her own. Her condition is called acute flaccid myelitis (AFM). Chloe uses a powered wheelchair and has a ventilator to help her breathe.

In the ICU, the doctors were telling me to get ready to take her home, but I refused. I wanted Chloe to go to an inpatient rehabilitation center so they could make her "better." I couldn't imagine the level of care she'd require. I told them, "I don't even water my own plants!"

Before Chloe was diagnosed with AFM, I had even worked for a nonprofit that helped people with special needs live and work in the community. I remember saying that I'd always applauded parents of kids who have special needs. I admired their dedication and ability to give their child a great life. I explained, though, that I'm just *not* that mom. After all, I fainted in high school biology class while dissecting a frog! I can't do this!

And despite my protests, I became *that mom*!

Chloe needed a lot of care from a variety of people, and I started to see what worked and what didn't. I started to ask questions of other parents of kids with special needs, too. Although I didn't get all the answers I needed, my intuition as Chloe's mom kicked in. Chloe, her twin brother, my husband, and I worked together to come up with good decisions for our family. I even got trained in all of Chloe's medical care. It took me a while, but I did it! I have come to realize that you may not be prepared for everything life throws at you, but you are stronger and smarter than you realize.

PUSHING ASIDE PERSONAL FEARS AND BIAS
by Andrea Saporito

Our younger daughter, Rachel, has dyslexia and mild attention deficit hyperactivity disorder (ADHD). When she was first assessed and diagnosed by a neuropsychologist, we were given two paths to consider. Option one, which was highly recommended, was to secure placement in an independent school that specializes in working with students with different learning disorders. Option two was to keep Rachel in public school and place her in an integrated co-teaching (ICT) class with a general and special ed teacher. We went with option two, which followed a more familiar path, and over the years, we hired tutors, psychologists, and executive function coaches to fill in the gaps the school couldn't provide.

Option two worked. Until it didn't. Rachel came home from the first day of seventh grade distraught. She was in the ICT class but had drawn the short straw on homeroom teachers. Homeroom, for a child with ADHD, is arguably one of the most important classes of the day. It is when a student needs to assess what notebooks and homework need to be in their backpack to bring home for the day to complete assignments. The new homeroom teacher had no experience working with children like Rachel, who needed extra guidance and support. Rachel was often unprepared in class while assignments sat in her locker, and by the end of the day, she would arrive home in tears. Whether entirely attributable to her homeroom teacher or not, Rachel's struggles were exacerbated by the situation.

Over the next six months, Rachel's dad and I focused on supporting Rachel as best we could, and while the COVID-19 pandemic upended all of our lives, we made the decision to apply to several of the independent schools we had previously rejected and secured a spot for the eighth grade.

Rachel now attends a school that is dedicated to the academic and social success of students with learning disabilities. The transformation in Rachel is extraordinary. Not only is she engaged with her schoolwork, she has finally formed meaningful friendships. Rather than crying and feeling frustrated, Rachel is happy and giggling with friends over the phone at all hours (okay, I don't love that part!).

Over the years, as we shuttled Rachel from tutor to tutor, I often wondered why we hadn't chosen to place her in one of the schools that had been recommended. If I am being honest, the words "special ed" came with too many negative connotations from our own childhoods. While the definition had evolved, Rachel's dad and I hadn't, and "special ed" wasn't a label we could reconcile with our vibrant, intelligent, and passionate child.

Looking back, perhaps we should have pushed aside our personal biases and fears earlier. I try not to have too many regrets, though, since when it mattered, we were ready and willing to make a different decision that was right for Rachel. And if we need to change directions again, I know we will. Until then, we will give ourselves some grace, enjoy watching Rachel shine at her new school, and be grateful it all worked out.

GIVING THE ULTIMATE GIFT
by Danielle Mirsky

When my son David was seven years old, he started to stumble on his words. Up until then, he spoke clearly and articulately. Over the course of a few months, however, saying each word aloud became a struggle. It was clear to me that David had developed a stutter. How long would it last? Is he nervous or anxious? Will it ever go away? I wondered aloud about all these things to my husband. He himself has a slight, not too noticeable stutter and said, "Well, the answer is no. He will have to learn how to live with it."

As the years progressed, David's stutter became more pronounced and definitely worse than my husband's mild stutter. When David met new people, it would take him no less than one full minute to say his name. He would also get stuck on each word when called on by his teacher in school. One teacher actually told me during our parent-teacher conference that she didn't have time to wait for David to get his words out, that he was holding up the lesson. So, we attempted to "help" in whatever way we could. We would finish his sentences when he was struggling, tell him to slow down, and make him practice speaking. But David's stutter prevailed, and it caused him to become more self-conscious and even shut down as he entered middle school.

While I wanted to take advantage of the individualized education plan (IEP) services to which David was entitled, I quickly realized the speech therapist was in over her head (which I discovered was not uncommon). I began to observe that many people who met David assumed he was nervous or there was something seriously wrong with him—simply because he was struggling to get a word out! David was also bullied, suffered from low self-esteem, and felt isolated. It became critical for him to learn to engage, interact, and understand who he was in the world. I knew it was essential for him to become resilient. It's not easy to teach this level of strength to a nine-year-old, however. We had a long road ahead.

After quite a bit of research, I was referred to a speech therapist who was well-experienced in stuttering. The first thing he taught David was to *own* his stutter. Essentially, when David met a new person, he needed to inform the other person that he stuttered to diffuse the situation. Then the speech therapist told us to wait for David to finish his sentences no matter how long it took. I can still hear him in my head. "Just be patient. He will get the words out." Lastly, the speech therapist referred us to an organization for kids who stutter, so David could meet other kids like him, express himself through theater, and know he was not alone. At first, David was hesitant. But the founder of the group was warm, understanding, and an all-around fun guy. It not only became the safe space for David and other kids who stuttered, but ended up being the sorely needed opportunity David had been missing in his life.

Lastly, we gave David the ultimate gift—weekly visits to a clinical psychologist. David was able to talk through his fears and successes with someone outside of his family without any angst around feeling judged.

Today David is not only thriving, he is even confident and unapologetic about his stutter. No, it did not go away, and it is something he continues to manage. But he accepts himself and understands that everyone has challenges they need to overcome. If that isn't resilient, I don't know what is.

THESE MOMENTS WILL MAKE YOU STRONGER
by Courtney Sochacki

My name is Courtney, and I am the mother of three sons, who are ten, eight, and five. Three and a half years ago, my middle son, Sawyer, was diagnosed with Duchenne muscular dystrophy. Duchenne is a progressive muscle disease in which typically boys will lose their ability to walk in middle school, and the usual life expectancy is in their twenties and thirties.

June 21, 2017, was the day life threw me that curveball. It took me about a month to digest the news of his diagnosis and decide I wasn't going to let that ball strike me out. Instead, I was going to swing for the fences!

I found that sitting around being sad wasn't helping me, my son, or our family. So I did some research and learned about the Muscular Dystrophy Association. I found that getting involved changed my outlook. The MDA gave me hope. But it also provided an avenue to raise money and pay it forward, joining so many parents before me who had paved the way. This isn't to say that getting involved made the diagnosis easier. I still had hard moments. I remember getting dressed for the first MDA gala and texting a friend, "I am not going, I can't do it." In response, she sent me a quote from Erin Van Vuren that I still read and reflect on quite often since it has gotten me through my darkest days: "There will be painful moments in your life that will change your entire world in a matter of minutes. These moments will change *you*. Let them make you stronger, smarter, and kinder. But don't you go and become someone that you're not. Cry. Scream if you have to. Then straighten out that crown, and keep moving."

I try to live by this and choose to ignore Sawyer's life expectancy. No one is promised tomorrow anyway. And just because we were given a crystal ball for my son's life doesn't mean it needs to consume me. I spent the first year or two after the diagnosis consumed with anxiety about what was going to happen, how we would adapt, and what would happen when Sawyer was eight (the age when a lot of kids start to use scooters). But here we are, and Sawyer is still a healthy eight-year-old who runs, jumps, and plays. Does he tire more quickly than his peers? Sometimes, but he is still living his life. Most important, I have tried to stop worrying about what the future will bring and live in the moment.

We recently had a snowstorm and were outside playing, when a bunch of teenage boys came back from sledding. At first, I thought to myself, "That will never be Sawyer." But then I snapped out of that quickly because *today* he was outside, playing and sledding.

I have learned to stay in the moment and live for today. I refuse to worry about what the future may hold because all that does is cause added stress and anxiety. Our experience has also caused me to take a step back and realize the world is still beautiful. Sometimes it's hard to watch your child get poked and prodded, spend countless hours at clinic appointments, and take more pills and vitamins than an adult. I remind myself that everything isn't always fair, and everyone has their cross to bear. But life is still beautiful.

PRIORITIZING SELF-CARE
by Katherine Kanaaneh

My son Tim is eighteen and was diagnosed with autism when he was three and a half years old. He has taken our family on a journey that has changed each of us in ways that we never could have imagined. He has limited verbal communication, seizures, and unpredictable behaviors that require constant supervision.

Tim is prone to wander off or swipe food (especially French fries) off anyone's plate with his ninja-fast reflexes. He likes to play in water, and when he was younger, would try to climb into fountains. Now he probably wouldn't climb into a fountain, but he would try to drink from it.

When he was younger, Tim would suddenly start laughing

hysterically, shout, or burp loudly. Between the loud noises, the wandering off, and eating strangers' food off their plates, family outings were not relaxing for me. Instead I found myself hypervigilant about keeping an eye on him, as well as tending to the rest of my family's needs. I felt sorry for myself.

But life has a funny way of putting inspiration right in front of you, and more than once it has come from other moms in my community. One summer, my daughter was on a soccer team and I met another mom from the team. She said her other child would need major physical support for the rest of his life, and she mentioned this to me in a casual way without complaint. Her happy demeanor as she shared a little bit of her life was eye-opening for me. I realized that I had been feeling sorry for myself, which wasn't helping me.

I thought how lucky that child was to have her as his mom, and I felt a shift within me. I realized that my outlook needed to change in order for me to be happier and to be a better mom. I started looking for ways to simplify my life and make self-care a priority. Self-care allows me to show up as the mom I want to be. I am now able to see and appreciate the positive things in my life and my son.

DON'T BE AFRAID TO MAKE A CHANGE
by Lesley Arlein

My name is Lesley, and my son is Jonah. When he was two months old, I noticed one side of his body appeared smaller than the other. His pediatrician diagnosed him with hemihypertrophy, an overgrowth disorder that causes the right side of his body to grow at a faster rate than his left. We were then referred to a geneticist. At five months old, Jonah was ultimately diagnosed with Beckwith-Wiedemann syndrome (BWS), a rare genetic disorder. For the next eight years, Jonah was screened for potential childhood tumors related to the disorder (which he thankfully never had). He continues to be followed by an orthopedist in anticipation of surgery to correct his leg-length difference.

Fast-forward thirteen years, in the midst of the COVID-19 pandemic and unrelated to his BWS, Jonah began having fevers, was lethargic, and seemed to have lost weight, among other ailments. I brought him to his pediatrician after he had expressed concern that he might have cancer. She didn't seem overly worried, and I almost felt silly for taking him to the doctor based on her reaction. But I still asked for them to perform thorough blood work to alleviate his fear. After taking Jonah to a gastroenterologist, within two weeks he was diagnosed with Crohn's disease, an autoimmune disorder that causes inflammation along the gastrointestinal tract.

After receiving Jonah's latest diagnosis, we didn't hear from his pediatrician at all. I had always felt a sense of loyalty to her, but now I knew it was time to rip the Band-Aid off and switch to a new pediatrician. As someone who has a difficult time changing hairdressers, I found it hard to "break up" with her. Given the newest challenges we were facing, though, Jonah needed a doctor who would be our quarterback, willing to help us coordinate our son's care with his multiple specialists. As my child's strongest advocate, I had to ignore my fears of change and my yearning to stick with what was familiar, knowing Jonah deserved more.

I wish I had made the change sooner and hadn't worried so much about everyone else's feelings. It felt like a tremendous weight had been lifted off my shoulders as soon as I finally made the decision. In the end, my family's well-being is most important.

THIS IS HIS JOURNEY
by Angie Armstrong

I am a mother of a girl and two boys. All three were born healthy and vibrant. My youngest by six years is Kobe, who has always been a bit more spoiled than the other two. But we loved how he completed our family, and life was great! I loved every moment of raising our kids.

When Kobe turned thirteen, we were on a summer vacation in Florida. On a lovely day, when the waves were perfect, Kobe was having a blast using his boogie board. He may have indulged in a few extra sodas, and certainly his sleeping pattern was not as it would have been if we were at home. But, hey, we were on vacation, and we allowed the kids to stay up late, eat junk food, and drink sodas. I had no reason to not allow this. Kobe was a healthy young boy!

But then, in the middle of the night, our daughter came running into our room, shaking and screaming that something was wrong with Kobe. My husband and I both ran into his room and saw him convulsing. His eyes were rolled in the back of his head, he had foam coming out of his mouth, and his body was jerking uncontrollably. Terrified, we immediately called 911. What was wrong with our son? As we rode in the ambulance to the nearest hospital, I could hardly breathe.

At the emergency room, they informed us that Kobe had a "grandma seizure," possibly due to dehydration from the sun, salt water, and tons of soda. They suggested he take an anti-seizure medication and that we follow up with his doctor as soon as we returned home. The rest of the vacation went on without a hitch.

I could not get the picture out of my head of my baby having a seizure, however. All I wanted to do was take him to the doctor and get him better. Because that is what moms do when their children are ill, right? Well, not this time. Kobe's seizures returned when we got home. After visiting multiple doctors and changing medications a few times, we decided to get a second opinion. We kept wondering whether we did something wrong on our vacation. Why was this happening? After many brain scans and several hospital stays, Kobe was eventually diagnosed with epilepsy. We prayed and prayed that his condition was caused by puberty and he would outgrow it. That day never came.

Kobe's invisible difference is unknown to most people around him. He also wears a medical bracelet at all times. Unfortunately, I'm afraid any time he is not with me. I make him give my number to every single person he leaves our house with. I feel the need to explain what to do with him if he were to have a seizure on their watch. This condition has changed our whole lives, not just Kobe's.

When it began, all I wanted was to talk with other moms

going through the same thing, but I couldn't find any. Many times, when Kobe was having a seizure, I would yell for my husband to come help, so I could secretly escape the room and cry profusely. I constantly felt like I had swallowed a handful of cotton balls and they were stuck. This feeling has never left me. I'm on edge when Kobe is away from me. If my phone rings, I just know it is someone on the other line informing me that he has had a seizure. I could not bring myself to think positively for a long period of time. If things are going well and it has been a while since the last seizure, I start thinking the worst. Unfortunately, Kobe has not been able to go six months without a seizure since this all began six years ago.

My concern now is, will he live with us forever? How can I let go of something I have no control over? I am his mom, so why can't I help him? As the years have progressed, I have been able to give myself some grace, but it has not been easy. I have come to the conclusion that at some point in time, Kobe must take the responsibility for being an epileptic and know that his actions and decisions in life need to be what is best for his health. And I must know that Kobe's decisions are his, not mine. As Kobe becomes a grown young man, I need to continually remind myself that this is his journey!

I LET MY INNER VOICE GUIDE ME
by Heather Garnett

In the wee hours of the morning, I had finally given birth to my second baby girl, Ava. I could faintly hear the nurse stating her weight. For a full-term baby, and taking into account my weight gain, it seemed very low. I was caught off guard, but then was reassured as she was placed in my arms while the nurse on call exclaimed, "She is perfect!" Perfect she was. But as I stared into the eyes of my sweet baby girl, I innately knew something was awry. Was it my mother's intuition? I really didn't know, but I just knew that something inside of me felt uncertain. Nevertheless, I was extremely exhausted and after over twelve hours of labor, I needed to rest. Ava was whisked away to the nursery.

After examining Ava the following morning, her pediatrician came into my hospital room and asked my husband and me to sit down. During the exam, he had noticed that Ava couldn't fully extend her arms, only to 80 degrees on her left arm and 75 degrees on her right arm. The pediatrician wasn't sure what her elbow contractures could be attributed to but also described her thumb, pointer, and middle fingernails as malformed. Although he'd seen this type of malformation of the nails before, he requested that Ava have an MRI, CT scan, and blood work completed. The test results would hopefully give us more answers.

Up until that morning, we were not aware that she was born with a limb difference. The three doctors who had examined her right after birth missed this staggering distinction. Upon hearing about these differences from her pediatrician, I promptly drifted into a state of shock and told my husband, "Do not say one word to anyone. Not our parents, not to anyone in our family, not to our friends." I couldn't handle the questions, and I wanted nothing more than to protect our sweet, innocent child.

But the doctors needed to complete further tests and it was almost unbearable to handle. A profound heaviness from fear and the unknown filled my heart.

After the multiple test results had given us no more answers than we started with, I built up a huge wall of protection. While trying to cope with her unknown diagnosis, I relied on my husband as my greatest confidant because he knew my fear, my grief, my anxiety, and the extreme love that I had for our child. I needed to keep everyone else, including my parents, in-laws, family members, and friends, at arm's length. While I knew they wanted to help, they were not what I needed at the moment, since I believed no one could understand what I was going through. In due time, I allowed others in, to hear our story—Ava's story. During this period, what I needed the most was time. My husband and I both needed time to process what was happening in our lives. I found it best to surround myself with people like my sister who would call me to ask, "Hey, how are you?" but also understood how relieved I was to change the subject by switching gears to things like "Guess what happened over here today?"

I made the decision to have my heart guide me in figuring out what my family and I needed. It was necessary for my mental health. Shockingly, it took almost ten years for the marker of nail-patella syndrome to be identified in our daughter's blood work. The wall of protection that I'd built to assist in figuring out how to best parent her made all the difference in the world. I listened to my inner voice and let it guide me. I could have easily fallen down the rabbit hole of fear. It took every ounce of strength that I had inside of me to reach out and ask as many questions as I could, to find the best care for my child.

At first my fear prevented me from speaking up about my daughter's care, but as time went on, I discovered the strength of my voice and the power of being her voice. In turn, Ava has grown to become her own greatest advocate.

ALL THINGS ARE RELATIVE
by Brian McKay

My son Davis was born with Down syndrome. My wife, Courtney, and I had done testing when she was pregnant, but the tests all came back as negative. When Davis was born, the nurse handed him to me and said, "He has some signs that he has some sort of syndrome." I asked, "Is it Down syndrome?" She replied that she couldn't say and that I would need to ask a doctor. What a shock and adjustment! All the dreams of having an ordinary child were gone. I wasn't sure if I was disappointed, scared, or both. I was sure that I didn't want Down syndrome in my life.

Of course, I learned how to accept it and worked on rebuilding my expectations for Davis. The thing about many kids with Down syndrome is that they don't perceive themselves as different. They don't even know they have it. Davis certainly doesn't.

Then in March 2013, when he was four, Davis was diagnosed with pre B-cell ALL (acute lymphoblastic leukemia). As the name states, it is acute and can be deadly within weeks. Suddenly, I realized that I did not care about DS. All I cared about was saving the life of my child. Down syndrome had taken a backseat.

Davis's treatment was four years long. We nearly lost him in the spring of 2016 to pneumonia. Thankfully, he's fully recovered from leukemia. Since then, Davis has become the light of our lives. He and his younger brother, Grant, have a beautiful and rich relationship. Davis is a bright spot in so many people's days. He has absolutely helped me become more accepting of all things unexpected and an advocate for the underprivileged and other-abled.

The phrase "all things are relative" is used frequently in our home when something bad or unexpected happens. No day will be as bad as the cancer diagnosis and no day will be as good as meeting "Big D" for the first time.

I NEEDED TO SLOW DOWN
by Judy Jenkins

My name is Judy, and most people who know me would agree that I set goals and work hard to achieve them. I could never have prepared for the journey of having a child with dyslexia, however. Never.

Claire, my middle daughter, has always been full of life. The meaning of Claire's name is "bright" or "clear," which fits her so well, even from the moment she was born. From a very early age, Claire loved illustrated books and would enjoy cuddling up to listen to me read. The pictures helped her create the story in her mind. Our bedtime rituals included bath time and a favorite book. When Claire was younger, I would read books like *Goodnight Moon* and not think twice that she was content as long as someone else was reading to her.

But when she started preschool and was expected to read, her happiness faded. Her struggles were real and so painful for me to watch. Every time Claire attempted to utter the words while trying to read, she'd fumble with the sounds. Reading came so naturally for young children her age. Why not for my daughter? We both became increasingly frustrated and she'd begin to cry whenever a book was in her hands.

Witnessing my daughter struggling to such an acute degree just made me try everything to help. I even transformed my kitchen into a word wall so Claire would regularly see the words. That seemed to be working, or so I thought. But I soon realized Claire possessed a phenomenal sight memory. Instead of relying on decoding strategies, Claire memorized all the words that engulfed our kitchen.

The taskmaster in me kept pushing Claire, but I didn't want to admit to myself that she had been pushed to her limits. One afternoon, when tears were streaming down Claire's cheeks as she was trying to read, she suddenly screamed aloud, "My brain feels like it is on fire!" That was the moment I was sure that my little Claire-Bear was dyslexic. It was also the moment that I put on the brakes. I had to come to terms with the fact that my efforts alone couldn't fix the issues she was having. As her mom, I also had to learn a vital lesson—I needed to slow down. Whatever help she needed wasn't something I alone could quickly fix.

Formal testing concluded Claire had dyslexia and attention deficit hyperactivity disorder (ADHD); then the search for finding the best for Claire began. With the right tutor and school, Claire progressed over time. Meanwhile, I began to accept that her strides often occurred outside the home, out of my control. Reflecting back on Claire's journey, I realized I'd originally thought she just couldn't take another step, exhausted by the level of mental energy required to overcome her challenges, and that I needed to be the one to help her. But once I let go, Claire got the help she needed. Most important, she has achieved a level of success I couldn't have predicted.

CHILD FIRST, SPECIAL NEEDS CHILD SECOND
by Julie Schlager

My husband, Dan, and I, both hearing, gave birth to two deaf children. I remember like it was yesterday the moment when we received the news that our one-month-old daughter had a profound hearing loss. I knew something was wrong before the hospital audiologist spoke—the test didn't seem to be yielding any results, but what did we know? We dared ask the doctor if our daughter would ever learn to talk. His answer was terrifying: "Likely never." In a state of complete shock, we got in the car and began driving.

That first hour was probably one of the most defining moments of our lives. Rather than focusing on the negative, I had two thoughts. The first was a feeling of fierce, protective, Mama Bear love. This child was going to be loved and cared for by us, and *no one* was going to diminish all the gifts she had. Dan and I decided immediately to do whatever it took—move to a community where people only signed, learn to sign ourselves, be involved in every activity needed to make it work, give up many of our dreams—to give our child what she needed. My second thought was to *not* consider this profoundly deaf diagnosis as a death sentence. I was looking at a beautiful baby. She could still be smart, athletic, curious, intellectual, independent, and ours. We could still share our lives, thoughts, loves, and many personality traits. She could still captain her soccer team. We could still ski together with her. She could be a good student—maybe in a different kind of school than I went to. The dream of us championing her, then her championing herself, and us being a close family team was born.

In the end, both our children learned to hear and speak well. They are amazing students, incredible artists, and team-playing athletes. Most important, they are kind, connected, independent, and happy. And we are that close family team I dreamed of, but Dan and I are only support staff now!

How did we get there? First and foremost, by slowly but persistently getting help, finding specialists, and learning about hearing loss. In our daughter's first eight years, we were in eight different programs, schools, and therapies, and saw many different doctors, specialists, and therapists. We kept learning and growing and pushing for what we wanted and believed was in our daughter's and son's best interests. We embraced a village of people who helped us! Second, we focused on all the other stuff in life, too: making friends, pursuing interests and activities, relaxing and leading "normal" lives—for both the kids and us. I know now that this was just as important as the "special needs" work.

In the end, the best piece of advice I ever received was this: *child first, hearing/special needs child second.*

Love your baby, rock your baby, feed them, diaper them, and snuggle them before you worry about the rest. Our job was *not* to raise "hearing impaired" kids but to raise "plain old" kids. And that is what we did.

RELAX AND EMBRACE HUMOR
by Ellen Ladau

My daughter, Emily Ladau, shares the same disability that I have: Larsen syndrome, a hereditary musculoskeletal disorder. We both have dislocated joints with limited range of motion and bone abnormalities. We are full-time wheelchair users. Larsen syndrome also can cause severe spinal abnormalities. Emily's abnormal curvature, called "kyphosis," put her at risk of quadriplegia or even death if her neck sustained an impact injury. Emily wore custom-made cervical collars and needed biannual MRIs to monitor whether her spinal cord was being compressed. Our life was a constant balancing act between exercising caution and allowing Emily the freedom to be a kid. The surgery to correct her spinal curve occurred when she was seventeen, and though we made it through, it was extremely rough on us all.

I know what you're likely thinking: "Wow, now here's someone who surely must have the secret sauce to parenting a disabled child!" Sorry to disappoint, but I don't. There is definitely no universal recipe to follow as a disabled parent or for parenting a disabled child that will guarantee perfect results every time. Needless to say, there is no such thing as perfect.

My longing to be overprotective of Emily was fiercely strong. But compartmentalizing became an essential strategy for me. A day with a medical appointment or surgeries clearly deserved my full attention. So I made it a point to try and relax and enjoy the other days on the calendar when we just lived our normal life. Easier said than done. But I learned it's okay to even laugh at some of the comical situations disability may bring. We do this often in our house, especially when no one is around to help us. The way Emily and I need to reach things or clean up spills usually puts us into fits of giggles. We also learn to positively spin the comments we inevitably get when we are in public. Much to Emily's chagrin, I never tire of being mistaken for her sister. She says it is our twin wheelchairs that cause this mistaken identity. I say it is my youthful appearance!

Now that Emily is an adult, I am happy to report that Emily and I are truly best friends. Not only has Emily become a disability rights activist and accomplished author, she proudly embraces her disability as part of her identity and has even helped me to do the same. I could not be more proud to be her mom.

ACKNOWLEDGMENTS

To Lisa Leshne, my literary agent. Before blowing out the candles on my fortieth birthday, I realized I had an urge . . . no . . . a deep yearning to write a book. Perhaps a memoir? Only, at that point, I had never written anything worth reading. I actually naïvely wondered if, Lisa, you signed me out of guilt simply because our families belonged to the same synagogue in central Illinois and we had been acquainted growing up. At our first lunch in Manhattan, you told me you had admired me from afar. I was taken aback since I had always felt the same about you. In many respects, your commitment to me was steeped in blind faith, and your constant support and involvement were vital in helping me redirect my approach. You taught me the value of building my platform, which I thought initially would solely help others. But it created a boomerang effect, further boosting my own emotional growth, which I used to support our own children even further. Not only did you motivate me to find my literary voice and encourage me to sharpen my writing chops, you knew intuitively that my personal experience could provide an enlightened understanding to so many. *Born Extraordinary* became a reality due to your unwavering confidence and belief in me. It is because of you, Lisa, that my wish came true. My most heartfelt gratitude also goes to Samantha Morrice at the Leshne Agency, for your own brilliant touch and enthusiastic optimism that we'd find it the perfect home.

To Peter and Ted Weinbaum, my brothers. The best way I can describe how much you've meant to me is that your involvement in my life inspired an entire chapter! You both always had my back and made sure I had exactly what I needed to succeed. May every kid who is different benefit from a family that helps them to take flight while simultaneously feeling grounded and loved. I adore and revere you both.

To Leslie and Lenny Zucker, my in-laws. Let's face it, you raised the most magnificent of men—John has the biggest heart, the quickest wit, and the strongest sense of self. Thanks to your unequivocal support, he joined me in this very wild and joyful ride, ready to tackle anything, even before I was prepared myself. From the beginning, you accepted me without hesitation and celebrated your grandchildren, something that any person who is different isn't guaranteed but deserves.

To Judy Fisher, my mentor. You believed my future would be bright even when it felt its darkest. Your mantra, "What you think of me is none of my business," inspired me to resist the judgment of others and was the key to conquering my fears. It allowed me and my children to live our lives to their fullest. I feel so thankful I've grown into the woman you were certain I'd become one day.

To Lauren Tarshis and Danielle Mirsky, my fairy godmothers. More than a decade ago, when my ideas to empower kids who are different were but merely a twinkle, you both instantly and wholeheartedly believed in me. Your ideas and foresight inspired me to shoot for things I hadn't even fathomed, and I'm forever indebted to and enamored of you both.

Acknowledgments

To RBC Foundation USA, Lauren Stanley, Daniel Vitaletti, Kiini Salaam, Jamie Engel, and Ann Amstutz Hayes, my support network. If you hadn't believed in my vision, I'd have missed out on the opportunity to start Don't Hide It, Flaunt It as a 501(c)(3) nonprofit organization. Your continued commitment allowed DHIFI to establish and grow its valuable empathy and social and emotional learning programs for kids, which expanded my own understanding and perspective. As a result, I've had the privilege of meeting a magnificent variety of people, some of whom have even contributed to this book. I am truly grateful.

To Bill Tabin and Jay Stark, my professional leaders at the Royal Bank of Canada. Your eager and unhesitating support as I followed this other labor of love has been such an important gift to me. You are responsible for both my professional fulfillment and freedom to be myself in the workplace.

To the phenomenal team at TarcherPerigee (Penguin Random House)—Joanna Ng, Marian Lizzi, Rachel Ayotte, Alyssa Adler, Viviana Moreno, and Katie MacLeod-English, my literary MVPs. Your faith in my vision and the inherent value of *Born Extraordinary* gave me the encouragement I needed to complete this labor of love. I will always cherish your commitment and support.

To Ethan, Charlie, and Savanna, my children. I don't take for granted your willingness to trust me to share our story. It is impossible to articulate the level of strength, wisdom, and comic relief all three of you have provided me. Being your mom has not only provided me immense joy, it has been my honor. I have learned the true meaning of unconditional self-love by being married to your dad and raising you. You are my proudest accomplishment.

ABOUT THE AUTHOR

A graduate of the University of Wisconsin–Madison and NYU School of Law, Meg Zucker is an attorney and leader in anti-money laundering and financial crimes on Wall Street. She is also the founder and president of Don't Hide It, Flaunt It® (DHIFI), a 501(c)(3) nonprofit organization whose mission is to advance understanding, tolerance, and mutual respect for people's differences. DHIFI provides "flaunt it" social and emotional learning and anti-bullying programming to public and private schools, universities, community service organizations, and diversity, equity, and inclusion programs at Fortune 500 companies. Meg is a high-demand speaker and activist. She has been featured on the *Today* show, Today.com, The Female Lead, and was the keynote speaker in the Distinguished American Speaker series in Tel Aviv, hosted by the U.S. ambassador to Israel. Meg's writing has appeared in *Parents* magazine, *USA Today*, *Scholastic Storyworks*, and *The Forward*, as well as online in Scary Mommy, Motherwell, and The Mighty. The Zucker family was the subject of a TLC special, *My Extraordinary Family*.